D0593628

THE
HOME UNIVERSITY LIBRARY
OF MODERN KNOWLEDGE

COMMUNISM

By

HAROLD J. LASKI

PROFESSOR OF POLITICAL SCIENCE
IN THE UNIVERSITY OF LONDON

THORNTON BUTTERWORTH, LTD.
15 BEDFORD STREET, LONDON, W.C.2

First Printed	. . . . .	*April,*	*1927*
Reprinted	. . . . .	*June,*	*1927*
Reprinted	. . . . .	*August,*	*1927*
Reprinted	. . . . .	*May*	*1928*

MADE AND PRINTED IN GREAT BRITAIN

TO

L. T. HOBHOUSE

AND

M. GINSBERG

PIGNUS AMICITIÆ

PREFACE

No book on communism can hope to be impartial, for its problems are too urgent not to involve some bias, however unconscious. I can only say that I have sought so to state the communist "theses" upon the topics I have discussed that its own advocates would (as I hope) recognise that even an opponent can state them fairly. Whenever italics are given in a quotation, they are reproduced from the original.

The bibliography has presented many difficulties. After many attempts I have simply given a list of books that are essential to the understanding of communism. For fuller references the bibliography cited will be found of great value.

I desire to acknowledge the help I have derived, in writing Chapter III, from the Master of Balliol's little book on Marx's *Capital*. I know no volume in English that better explains the purpose and limitations of its theme.

H. J. L.

The London School of Economics
and Political Science.
1st December, 1926.

CONTENTS

Among volumes of kindred interest already published in The Home University Library are :—

No. 1. *Parliament.* By Sir C. P. Ilbert.

No. 10. *The Socialist Movement.* By J. Ramsay MacDonald, M.P.

No. 11. *Conservatism.* By Lord Hugh Cecil, M.P.

No. 21. *Liberalism.* By Professor L. T. Hobhouse.

No. 96. *Political Thought in England*—From Bacon to Halifax. By G. P. Gooch, M.A.

No. 104. *Political Thought in England*—From Herbert Spencer to the Present Day. By Ernest Barker, M.A.

No. 106. *Political Thought in England*—The Utilitarians from Bentham to J. S. Mill. By W. L. Davidson, M.A.

No. 121. *Political Thought in England*—From Locke to Bentham. By Professor Harold J. Laski.

COMMUNISM

CHAPTER I

INTRODUCTORY

I

Communism has become, in our own day, at once an ideal and a method. As an ideal, it aims at a society in which classes have been abolished as a result of the common ownership of the means of production and distribution. As a method, it believes that its ideal can be attained only by means of a social revolution in which the dictatorship of the proletariat is the effective instrument of change.

As an ideal, communism has an honourable tradition which reaches back to the very beginnings of Western political thought. The *Republic* of Plato already envisages a communist State; and, since his day, there has hardly been a generation in which some thinker, oppressed by the social consequences of private property in the means of production, has not sought to remedy them by its abolition. All political literature, indeed, until the Reformation, is full of doubts of the moral validity of private property; it is only since that time that economic individualism, in any full and unmitigated sense, has asserted its full sway over the minds of men. For the previous eighteen hundred years, the Stoic notion of the equality of mankind deposited an uneasy belief that its consequences should manifest themselves in the sphere of economic fact. That there was communism in the golden age was taken almost for granted; and when that period was equated by Christianity with the time before the Fall, what was to become the classic theology of Western Europe became impregnated with a similar faith. Accordingly, the Roman Lawyers, the New Testament, the early Fathers and the mediæval Schoolmen all found it difficult to defend an economic system in which some men could suffer from privation, while others prospered. If most took refuge in the facile and convenient doctrine of stewardship, and accounted for private property by the tragedy of the Fall, there remained many who could not suffer this compromise. Nor did the modified Aristotelian view of Aquinas find universal favour. The mediæval records contain indubitable traces of men and sects, often obscure enough, who preached a thoroughgoing communism. The strict followers of St. Francis, the Beguins and the Beghards, John Ball and his disciples in 1381, are merely examples of a widely-spread temper. It is not too much to say that at every mediæval period of social crisis, some men will be found to declare that the only radical cure for oppression is the abolition of private property.

Yet we must not make too much of this mediæval communism. For the most part, and naturally enough, it is less a coherent body of social doctrine than a reflection of the otherworldliness of the Middle Ages. That is obviously the case with the oft-discussed communism of Wycliff; the friend of John of Gaunt cannot seriously be regarded as the considered ally of social revolution. What we are confronted with is rather a fine distaste for materialism, a sense that the rich man cannot enter the kingdom of heaven, a *cri de cœur* against the rigidity of feudal structure, than a genuine social philosophy.

Much the same is true of communist teaching in the period between the Reformation and the French Revolution. That of Sir Thomas More is clearly no more than the attractive fancy of a great humanist, depressed by the economic evils of the time. Gerard Winstanley and his disciples in Cromwellian England, indeed, represent a genuinely communist view. " From each according to his powers, to each according to his needs " is no unfair summary of the *Law of Freedom in a Platform* (1652). Co-operative production, the abolition of exchange, the idea of the necessary quota of labour which each must perform under penalty, all the regular incidents of Utopian communism are there. But Winstanley, like so many idealists, is clearer about the aims he has in view, than the methods by which he proposes to attain them. He realised the importance of education, and the study of natural science; he has that sense of the possibility of changing human nature which is the foundation of reforming creeds. But the inner light which drew him to Quakerism did not shine brightly among the practical Puritans of his day; and his little band of Diggers on St. George's Hill are important in the history of thought rather than of action.

We cannot here seek to narrate the history of communism before the Industrial Revolution; it must suffice merely to give instances of the permanence of the ideal. That the grim economic facts of eighteenth-century France should have led men of sensitive temper to this view is intelligible enough; the contrast between the extremes of luxury and poverty was too glaring for its meaning to be missed. The poor parish priest Meslier, for example, was driven to communism by the horrors he encountered among his flock. "You are amazed, O ye poor," he cried, "that ye have so much evil and suffering in your lives, . . . if, as I desire, all possessions were common, there would be no taxes to fear." Meslier protests with bitterness against the monstrous tyranny under which society groans; and he sees no remedy save in revolution. But he has little to say of its coming save to urge that men have the power in their hands if they will but show the courage and the will. His *Testament* is the protest of a noble soul, tormented by the evils of his time; but it is the book of a moral prophet rather than of a social analyst.

In a less degree, this is true, also, of Mably and Morelly. The latter, of whose life practically nothing is known, presents us with a complete scheme of communism, elaborate in groundwork and detail, in his *Code de la Nature* (1755); but the work is interesting rather for its emphasis upon the moral superiority of communism over individualism, and the amazing power of imaginative detail that it reveals, than for any profound insight into the nature of social change. Mably is a more considerable figure. The brother of Condillac the philosopher, and the disciple of Rousseau, he is as noteworthy for character as for ability. The idea of equality was his passion, and it is because a system of economic equality would prevent the degradation of human impulses that he decides upon its necessity. No one has pointed out more clearly the evils that follow in the train of inequality; and he believes that Sparta and Paraguay prove that private property is unnecessary. "The state as universal owner," he wrote, in his *Doutes aux Economistes*, "will distribute to each citizen the possessions he needs." But Mably has no knowledge of how the change may be effected. A revolution may be necessary; between the slavery of the present and a violent upheaval to secure a better future, he sees no middle term. Yet in his counsel to the Poles, who sought his advice, it is upon the slow process of inevitable change that he seems to depend. A revolution, he says, is possible in a small State, if there is a Lycurgus, but upon no other condition. He can propose, as a *pis aller*, reforms in which the right to individual property is so organised as to minimise its inevitable evil. He remains, however, pessimistic of the outcome; and, unlike his master Rousseau, he does not disguise his fears in magnificent declamation.

The benefits of economic equality were a commonplace among the advanced social theorists of France in the eighteenth century; though few had the hardihood to go so far as communism. A vague socialistic view is general; it affects alike Montesquieu and Rousseau, the Encyclopedists and the more radical of the clergy. But it remains, inevitably, a doctrine without substantial power. Nor is it confined to France. Men like Ogilvie and Spence in England make it clear that the tradition is widespread; and the *Political Justice* of Godwin (1793) is, like the *Code de la Nature* of Morelly, a fully-developed communist philosophy. Its thesis is a simple one. Private property, says Godwin, means inequality, and inequality destroys the chance of moral and intellectual progress. Where there is wealth, there is pride and ostentation, vanity and corruption, while poverty is the nurse of a slave-mentality. Godwin has no special end or method to recommend. Opposed in principle to coercion, he desires a revolution in the mind only; and it is because material possessions hinder the free play of reason that he seems to resent them. His book, as Pitt saw, was not likely to inflame the masses; and if it inspired the poets to sing its influence was rather, as Wordsworth said in the *Prelude*, that "a strong shock was given to old opinions" than in any specific influence upon its age. It trained men's minds in new directions, and in this sense was a powerful dissolvent; but it did not make men communists, since it was rather an ethical than a political treatise.

The difficulty, indeed, with all communistic thought before the Industrial Revolution, lay in the material with which it had to deal. The obvious evils felt by men were political rather than economic in nature. The structure of industry was still too primitive and atomic for the appeal to be other than an individual one. The economic evils of a system which divides the social order into rich and poor were clearly seen. But the changes urged were moral ideals rather than social methods; and where, as with Meslier, revolution is postulated, it is more the prediction of angry despair than the outcome of a deliberate insight into social process. We are still dealing with a political philosophy whose substance is theological in texture.

II

The Industrial Revolution, by changing the mechanisms of production changed also the perspective of social philosophy. The people were herded into factories, and the division of society into masters and men became the outstanding index to social categories. The new production made combination inevitable, and, with the coming of combination, the development of a theory of mass-action became essential. For the individual suffered eclipse; he was submerged into that group within the social order to which, as Burke would have said, a divine tactic had assigned him. The result is seen in the new economics of which Ricardo, rather than Adam Smith, is the founder. Not, indeed, that the vision is confined to England. Hodgskin, Thompson, and Bray are, in purpose, though not in technique, paralleled by the Utopian socialists of France. But because the Industrial Revolution found its primary completion in England, it was in England that there developed the first organised philosophy of revolt.

As the Napoleonic wars drew to their close the whole generation turned its mind to economic questions. "Man," wrote Isaac D'Israeli, with indignation, "is considered only as he wheels on the wharf, or spins in the factory." What Mr. Tawney has called the Acquisitive Society unfolds itself before us. If some were intoxicated by the new vision of unlimited wealth, others were not wanting to insist that, in its production, labour was the sole or, at least, the principal factor. Labour, accordingly, was robbed. The exploitation of the new capitalists is the main theme of radical speculation after 1815. It produced the moral communism of Owen. Thomas Hodgskin drew from it the vital principle that trade unions are essentially fighting organisations for the defence of labour; though, rather surprisingly, he ends with a plea not for socialism, but for the individual right to property. With J. F. Bray, it leads to a passionate demand that the workers, through their trade unions, and by political agitation, shall accomplish their emancipation; and the end he has in view is Owenite communism. Indeed, English social history from 1815 until 1846 is a period of revolutionary fervour. The sense that labour was robbed was everywhere widespread and deep. The combination of economic oppression and political injustice, which produced the Grand National Consolidated Trades Union of the Owenites, the demand for a general strike from Benbow, and the Chartist Movement, is proof of how deep was the *malaise*. There are few modern ideas not discoverable in the epoch. Syndicalism, socialism, communism, universal suffrage as the means to the capture of political institutions, anarchism as the ideal when capitalism has been overthrown, the general strike as the demonstration of labour's solidarity and power, all of them were there. What was lacking was precision of method, on the one hand, and a massive analysis of facts on the other. The early English socialists are almost luxurious in suggestion. The end they envisage is clear; the cause they have at heart is set out with great ability and passionate conviction. What it still lacks is transference to the plane of universality. It is not yet either a philosophy of history, or a method evolved from that philosophy. It remains, above all, an eloquent confusion of great ideas.

Nor did France supply the necessary motive-power. Important as is the work of Saint-Simon, Fourier, Proudhon and Louis Blanc, it cannot be said that they made, in any ultimate way, the outlines of a communist philosophy. Saint-Simon saw, with incomparable insight, the importance of the new industrialism; Fourier emphasised the danger to society of a proletariat without interest in its maintenance; Proudhon—a revival of whose influence is a peculiar feature of modern French social thought—emphasised in his own way what a disciple has happily termed a socialism for peasants; Louis Blanc defined an end to be reached by universal suffrage and the capture of the bourgeois State. Each of them is full of brilliant insight into the nature and limitations of the new capitalism. Much of what they had to say anticipates all the outstanding features of the later Marxian hypotheses. The sense of an unbridgeable chasm between rich and poor, the idea of labour exploited by the merciless capitalist, the theory of a class war, the danger of an unpropertied proletariat, the growing dependence of the small manufacturer upon the large combination, all of these conceptions were utilised by the French thinkers who sought to analyse the new society about them. But there is in the case of each a chasm between the end they have in view and the means of its attainment. Each of them has a clear view of what he ultimately desires. Few of them know how to relate the ideal to the structure of grim fact. It was easy to say, with Constantin Pecquer, that the socialisation of production is the sole way to avoid a new industrial feudalism. What they did not do was to produce a philosophy of history that could be used at once as a criterion of method and an explanation of social change. To have done this was the achievement of Karl Marx, and the history of communism after his advent assumes a totally different character because of his work.

III

From whatever aspect it be regarded, the work of Karl Marx is an epoch in the history of social philosophy. It is easy to show that he was less original than he believed, and that his debts to his predecessors were greater than he was anxious to admit. The vital fact about him is that he found communism a chaos and left it a movement. Through him it acquired a philosophy and a direction. Through him, also, it became an international organisation laying continuous emphasis upon the unified interest of the working-classes of all countries. The essence of Marx's work lies not in any special economic doctrine so much as in the spirit by which his total accomplishment was informed. He was the first socialist thinker to realise that it was less important to draw up the detailed constitution of Utopia than to discuss how the road thereto may be traversed. He was the first, also, to understand that the discovery of the road depended upon the detailed analysis of the environment about him. Marx wrote at once the epitaph of the new capitalism and the prophecy of its ultimate outcome. The first aspect of his work, both by reason of the materials he used and the theses he deduced from them, put the defenders of economic individualism finally upon the defensive; the second provided an inspiration to his followers which has increased in profundity as the years have gone by. It may be true that Marxian economics is in no small degree self-contradictory and it is certainly true that much of the Marxian sociology bears the obvious stigmata of its special time. Yet even when criticism has done its worst, the influence of the man and his doctrine remains enormous; and nothing so well explains the nature of communism as a consideration of his effort and its aftermath.

Marx was born in 1818, the son of a middle-class Jewish family converted to the Christian faith. After a university career, where he did brilliantly, he looked forward to an academic career; but his views had already become too radical for the authorities, and after a short period of journalism in Prussia, he was driven as an exile to Paris in 1843. There he met the French socialists, among them Proudhon, and, most notably, Frederick Engels, with whom he laid the foundations of an historic friendship. Driven from France in 1845, he went to Brussels, where he lived until the outbreak of revolution in the *annus mirabilis* 1848. That stay is notable for his final break with the French socialist tradition by his publication of an attack on Proudhon, the *Misère de la Philosophie* (1847), which is fatal to the latter's system. In the Brussels period, also, he became acquainted, through Engels, with the League of the Just, whose transformation into the League of Communists was made in the summer of 1847. It was for the second congress of this League, in December of that year, that Marx produced the classic document of communism in the famous *Manifesto*. Hardly was it complete when the outbreak of revolution summoned him to Paris. He did not stay there long; for with members of the League of Communists he was, in June, editing a revolutionary journal, the *Neue Rheinische Zeitung*, in Cologne. The articles he wrote for this paper are of great importance, since they foreshadow in some detail the strategy of modern communism. But the movement was before its time. Reaction in Germany was followed by repression in France; and in the summer of 1849 Marx found himself in London, a penniless exile, without prospects or hope. In London he remained until his death in 1883.

The thirty years of his English exile have something of epic quality about them. Though he was helped by Engels from time to time, and was for ten years the poorly paid correspondent of the *New York Tribune*, it was not until the late 'sixties that Marx's circumstances allowed him even the elementary comforts of life. They were years of immense labour. Long hours of research in the British Museum alternated with struggles against the suspicions and jealousies of other exiles. The writing of *Das Kapital* had to find its place amidst the labours, at no time easy, of founding the first International, and the composition of a large number of pamphlets, some of which, like the defence of the Paris Commune and the criticism of the Gotha programme, are amongst the most important of his works. His health, moreover, was always bad, and a temper at no time easy to live with had to adjust itself to continuous struggles with the divergent needs of Proudhonists and the adherents of Bakunin. Yet with all the difficulties he had to encounter, his death was in no sense premature; he had, as Liebknecht said at his graveside, "raised social democracy from a sect or school to a party." He was, of course, greatly aided by the circumstances of his time; and the colleagueship of men like Engels meant aid more precious than is often received in a political movement. But the history of socialism in the second half of the nineteenth century is so emphatically the history of Marx and his influence that, apart from him, the movement has little meaning of universal quality. To understand, therefore, the events which grew out of his labours, it is necessary to set them in the perspective of his essential ideas.

Marxism as a social philosophy can be most usefully resolved into four distinct parts. It is, first and foremost, a philosophy of history; and, arising from that philosophy, it is a theory of social development intended to guide the party of which he was a leader. Marx, in the third place, outlined a tactic the influence of which has been of special significance in our own day; himself an uncompromising agitator, he had reflected, as few agitators have the leisure to reflect, upon the adjustment of means to ends. He was, finally, an economic theorist, who sought, upon the basis of the classical economics, to transform its hypotheses into arguments which justified his own philosophy of action. For Marx himself, of course, none of these aspects is properly separable from any other. They form a logical whole, the unity of which he would have passionately defended. It is, however, possible to reject the validity of his economic system, while accepting the large outlines of his social theory. The later chapters of this book will attempt, in some detail, the examination of the whole structure. Here, it is only necessary to explain the bearing of his ideas in order to show the results to which they were related.

The Marxian philosophy of history is the insistence that the primary motive force in social change is the system of economic production which obtains at any given time. To its needs, all other forms of social effort will adjust themselves, whether consciously or unconsciously. Law, religion, politics, philosophy, all these are born of the reaction upon the human mind of the methods by which men wrest from nature the necessary means of life. Clearly, therefore, those who control the means of production occupy in society a place of special power. Their interest determines the distribution of the product. They make rules of social conduct which are adapted to the service of their interest. But this governing class, whatever the period under review, has not the interest of the community as a whole at heart. Society is divided always into those who control and those who are controlled; at the basis of the community lies the division of classes. It is the Marxian view that the struggle between classes is the vital factor in accelerating social change. As the feudal system became obsolete, the new commercial bourgeoisie struggled with the old landowning class for the control of the State. The Industrial Revolution signalised the triumph of the former, and it is in its turn engaged in a similar struggle with a wage-earning class which has no interest in common with its masters. For while the wage-earners are primarily concerned to sell their labour as dearly as they can, the master desires its purchase at the lowest possible price. And since the wage-earner must sell his labour or starve, the master, who, as the owner of capital, can afford to wait, is in a position to oppress the wage-earner in a way that makes the antagonism between them fundamental. Only, therefore, by the abolition of the master-class is it possible to resolve the conflict.

How is this abolition to be effected? It is

here that Marx made his own original and essential contribution both to social theory and political strategy. The antagonism between classes in the bourgeois State results in the development of trade unions. As these come to realise that their subjection is simply the result of the capitalist system, they become conscious that the interests of their class are one and indivisible. They realise that their combined power would enable them to overthrow the system of private ownership and establish a society in which the means of production belong to its members as a whole. They become, accordingly, increasingly hostile to the existing social order. They refuse to be satisfied with small concessions, and insist upon taking power into their own hands. There then develops the decisive struggle with the master-class, which, to retain its own power, will stop at no means, however foul. The workers must retort in kind. They must seize the State and establish a dictatorship of the wage-earners to secure the transition from capitalist to communist society. The period will inevitably be marked by bloody conflict, since a class does not peacefully acquiesce in its own suppression. The rôle of the class-conscious workers in this period is as much as possible to abridge it by their determination and courage. It would be a simple misreading of history on their part to believe that the masters can be persuaded into surrender.

All of this is, of course, a complete social doctrine, in which the economic theories of Marx are interesting without being integral. But a word upon them is useful, since they throw light upon his underlying view. Basing himself upon the Ricardian definition of value as the product of labour, Marx saw that labour must produce more than it receives. Labour, accordingly, is robbed by the capitalist since it receives only the price it can command in the market, while the surplus, however large, goes to the master. The purpose of socialism is to compel the reversal of this position. This becomes possible by the inherent contradiction of the capitalist régime. The growing poverty of the workers, the increasing concentration of capital in a few hands, the consequent depression of the small capitalist into a dependent of the master-class, the extension of the market to the whole world as a unit, with the resultant solidarity of labour the world over—all of this secures the "death-knell of capitalist private property." "The monopoly of capital," wrote Marx, "becomes a fetter on the mode of production. . . . Centralisation of the means of production and socialisation of labour finally reach a point where they become incompatible with their capitalist integument. This integument is burst asunder. . . . The expropriators are expropriated."

IV

So bare a summary, of course, does less than justice to the wealth of knowledge and ability with which the argument is advanced. But it will suffice if it serves to clarify the history of the doctrine in action. Broadly speaking, that history is now some sixty years old, and is divisible, with reasonable clarity, into two periods. In the first, which ended with the outbreak of war in 1914, socialism was waging a purely propagandist war. It was the outlook of small minority-parties in each country of importance; and even where, as in Germany, it had become a party of significance in the State, its growth was rather the expression of general discontent with existing governments, than of a belief in socialist principles. Nowhere had it seized the reins of power; nowhere, also, had it freed itself from a belief either in the virtues of nationalism, on the one hand, or of a conviction that revolution lay in the womb of some distant future, on the other. Socialists talked, indeed, of revolution, but not as men either prepared or determined to make it.

The war, in this aspect, altered the whole perspective of men's ideas. It revealed the weakness of the existing régime the world over. Socialism became the creed of millions who before had been content with the milder doctrines of pacifist liberalism. The outbreak of revolution in Russia, the capture of the Russian State by Lenin and the Bolsheviks, their maintenance of power in the face of attack from the rest of Europe, accelerated enormously the development towards a new era. Russia made it evident that Marx was no mere doctrinaire but the expositor of a faith that could be translated, however unexpectedly, into action. With the defeat of Germany, socialism entered into the stage of offensive conflict. It became the essential opposition in all civilised States except upon the American continent. Even the collapse of the parliamentary régime, as in Italy and Spain, only meant those dictatorships of capital which Marx himself had foreseen. On the long view, we seem, at least in Europe, to have entered upon that final period of class-antagonism, of which, in the Marxian view, the inevitable end was the communistic State. Nor are observers wanting to insist that the development, in America and the Far East, of a similar condition is likely rather to be postponed than avoided.

All this is, of course, an excessive simplification of the facts; and it will be necessary, as the argument develops, to revise certain of its affirmations in the light of possibilities of which either Marx did not conceive or which have won new significance that he could not have foreseen. But it is on any view the fact that any impartial mind must admit that the whole character of social demand has changed. We have reached a period in which the deliberate use of the machinery of the State for the mitigation of social inequality is obviously demanded. We have realised that the existence of a nation divided permanently into rich and poor is incompatible with the attainment of social justice. The choice before us is one of concessions by the governing class on a scale larger than in any previous period of history, or the overthrow of the social order by men who deny the validity of its foundations. That a peaceful compromise may be effected here and there is, clearly, possible enough; Marx himself recognised the possibility of such a compromise, as a transition, in England. But no one assuredly is to-day entitled to argue, at least if he is careful of the facts, either that revolution is impossible, or that revolution is not the inevitable outcome of organised resistance to any vital change. It is in this light that we must examine the recent evolution of socialist history.

It is unlikely that most of those who, on September 25th, 1864, met at St. Martin's Hall, Long Acre, had any notion of the significance of their Assembly. Its English protagonists, stout trade union radicals like George Howell and Odger, saw in it little more than a method of introducing English labour organisation upon the Continent. For Mazzini and his adherents it was to be the germ of an international and secret society of republicans, and when his view failed, he withdrew from association and support. To Marx alone does it seem to have presented itself from the outset as a union of the proletariat of all countries with the deliberate aim of emancipating the working-class. Its early history was in any case somewhat stormy and diversified; and the discussion of abstract ideas such as the social influence of religion gave the good Howell ample cause to fear that a programme would be drawn up which "the good conscience" of "a Bright or a Gladstone" could not accept. Yet, though in its first few years the International displayed more than the usual pangs of socialist travail, it was clear when it met in Geneva in 1866 that it fulfilled a real want. It had, indeed, already shown signs, in the expulsion of Blanqui and his followers, of that internal doctrinal dissension which was to lead to its downfall. But seventeen English trade unions had joined; and the second Trade Union Congress, in 1869, recommended membership to all affiliated organisations. It could, of course, do little more than pass pious resolutions on such matters as the shorter working-day and the necessity of destroying the Russian Tsardom; though it is evident that its mere existence terrified the political police of the Continent, and resulted in a real growth of trade unionism there. It was, however, too much a combination of political and industrial units with different purposes, the one having definite revolutionary aims, while the other sought merely the normal ends of trade unionism. And the different nations represented were upon the most varied levels of class-consciousness. The Swiss were individualist radicals; the Belgians had a doctrine of their own, akin to that of Proudhon; the French, as stout Proudhonists, were hostile to state-action. From an amalgam so varied, it was difficult to make a single goal the end.

After 1868, the signs of disintegration grew more intense. The addition to the International of the Germans resulted in the defeat of French proposals on Proudhonist lines. That phantasy had hardly been expelled when Bakunin and his friends made their appearance. The energy and enthusiasm of the Russian revolutionist can hardly be questioned; but he was a man without vision or mind. He was, moreover, notoriously unstable and secretive; underground intrigue was the very breath of his nostrils. To a mind like that of Marx, essentially the German *gelehrte*, Bakunin with his unscientific and haphazard dogmatism, was necessarily abhorrent. The International, indeed, grew, and even developed branches in America; but it was obvious that two such dominating temperaments as Marx and Bakunin could not co-operate together. They had different aims and different methods. The one desired a unified and central direction with the capture of the State for revolutionary ends; the other sought to make the International a federation of autonomous bodies aiming everywhere at anarchism. The conflict between them destroyed the International; for so strong and bitter was their antagonism that whole nations were enlisted on either side. In 1872, on the motion of Marx, it was decided to transfer the headquarters to New York. That was, of course, to destroy any prospect of European influence; and one can only suppose that Marx, ill and disillusioned, had come to believe that the International had outlived its usefulness. It lingered on for a little in New York, and actually held a congress in Geneva in 1876. But the vitality of the movement was gone, and when, at the Philadelphia Congress of 1876, only one European delegate attended, the General Council was abolished, and the first International was quietly interred.

Yet two great facts stand out in its history which, despite many of the miserable features which destroyed it, prevent its dismissal as futile. The first is the fact that to its work is directly traceable the conversion of the European working-classes to socialism. After the Congress of 1869, when resolutions in favour of the nationalisation of land were carried, a cleavage appears, which has become permanent, between the bourgeois parties of the left and socialist parties. The one group may aim at transformation; the other aims at revolutionary transformation. This cleavage was the work of the International's propaganda, and through that instrument, of Marx himself. Upon its wisdom, opinions may differ; but, from any standpoint, it was at once an achievement of world import, and a striking tribute to Marx's powers as an agitator.

The second fact is the Paris Commune of 1871. Few events in modern history have been more unjustly treated, even by liberal-minded writers. So far from being, as it too often appears in the books, the desperate attempt of a few ruffians, the Commune was essentially a foreshadowing of the Bolshevik Revolution, led, in the main, by leaders of the International, built upon a coherent body of social doctrine, and futile only because, premature as it was, it lacked the revolutionary energy of purpose which could alone have been attended with success. Its history has been written with great insight and sympathy by Marx, even though he regarded the attempt as ill-considered. His pamphlet was an official publication of the International, and led to the withdrawal therefrom of the English representatives upon its council. To understand his point of view, it is necessary to remember that, for the International, the Franco-German war was simply a dynastic adventure from which it stood aside; important, indeed, in that it showed how the necessity of war was secreted in the interstices of capitalism, but unrelated to the interests of the working-class. It should be borne in mind also, that the work of the International had transformed the French trade union movement from a body of craft-workers to a federation committed to Marxian socialism, convinced of the need for revolution, and of the opinion that defeat in war, with its consequent disillusion, offers the most favourable moment for its inception.

From this point of view, failure as it was, it is impossible to overestimate the significance of the Commune. Previous revolutions had been made within the categories of the existing economic system; that of 1871 sought, above all, to shatter the economic system itself. And because it aimed its main blow at the idea of private property, it was met with a repression which, considering the scale of the struggle, was as brutal as any in the historic record. Roughly speaking, the Commune demonstrated for revolutionary socialists six fundamental theorems. It showed, first of all, that it is not enough merely to seize the existing machinery of the State; for the purpose of revolution this must be shattered and replaced by more suitable forms. The army, moreover, must become an instrument of the proletariat, and not merely the chance and mercenary instrument of the government of the day; it is a weapon of danger unless it is permeated by revolutionary ideas. The old official class, thirdly, must disappear; the civil service must be replaced by men who hold office by the will of the party that has seized power. Nor must the mere capture of authority be regarded as the end of the revolutionary task. The lesson of the Commune is the need for dictatorship. The capitalist class must be repressed, and the dictatorship must continue to use stern measures until the final triumph of its purposes is assured; in this transition period democratic socialism is impossible. The authority of government is, therefore, handed over from organs claiming to be above society to its responsible servants; it is, that is to say, the exclusive and necessary appanage of the party making the revolution. Parliamentarism, finally, must be abolished. In its place must be established "a working corporation, legislative and executive, at one and the same time." "In the parliamentary system," wrote Lenin, "the actual work of the State is done behind the scenes, and is carried out by the departments, the chancelleries and the staffs; Parliament itself is given up to talk for the special purpose of fooling the 'common people.'" In place of this "incessant quadrille," there will be representative institutions, indeed, but institutions in which the members of the legislative assemblies are themselves submitted to the "armed vanguard of all the exploited and labouring masses."[1]

How far this analysis is legitimate, we may discuss later. Here it is sufficient to note that the failure of the Commune marks the end of an epoch. After 1871, and until 1914, the working-class was, for the most part, engaged in a peaceful development of its power. It was clear that the State was too strong to be destroyed by sudden attack, made without preparation. Revolution for the time being was abandoned, and, as socialist parties attained significance in Parliaments, was replaced by the search for possible mitigations of the capitalist régime. The growth of capitalism, indeed, especially in the guise of imperialism, seemed to suggest that the day of its end was far distant. Everywhere there grew up reformist socialism, representatives of which were even willing, like Millerand and Viviani in France, to take part in capitalist governments; and the trend of economic facts led many, of whom the German socialist, Bernstein, was the most notable, to assert that they had made the Marxian hypotheses obsolete. Certainly, the outbreak of war in 1914 found a European socialism almost wholly devoid of fighting authority.

[1] *The State and Revolution,* by N. Lenin (English translation), pp. 38–56.

V

The institutions of internationalism in the period between 1876 and 1914 were, indeed, typical of reformist socialism. The International, which was revived in 1889, was little more than a negotiating bureau, through which congresses were organised to pass resolutions. Its members were the national socialist parties, some of which were then hardly more than socialist in name, and all of which were too infected by nationalistic sentiments to be willing to co-operate for a common end. They were dominated by the German Social Democrats, who were officially Marxist; but their socialism did not mean much more than a profound hostility to war, and a vague insistence that it should be ended speedily and the crisis utilised to bring about the fall of capitalist supremacy. The resolution was simply a pious hope; for no measures of any kind to give effect to it had been thought out, and when the crisis did come, it found international socialism ineffective and unprepared. It resolved that the war was unnecessary and iniquitous, but most of its leading figures, while avoiding the cruder patriotism of the capitalist parties, united with the latter in its prosecution, and even direction.

To the communist, indeed, the position

created by the war was radically different from the view of it taken by the reformist socialists. To him, the war was simply the inevitable result of competing capitalisms in their imperialist guise; and imperialism was, in its turn, the expiring effort of nationalist capitalism to postpone its inevitable disintegration. Whether one capitalist imperialism triumphed over another was to him a matter devoid of importance. His task was to utilise the great crisis produced by the war to point out to the workers the significance of the position. The capitalist State had been, in his view, undermined at its base; consolidated revolutionary effort would secure its overthrow. To the communist, therefore, the situation was similar to that which confronted the Communards of 1871, even if the theatre of events was upon a vastly greater scale. The question of essential import was to use to the full the opportunity so uniquely afforded. Capitalism, as Marx had foreseen, had become its own grave-digger; was the working-class prepared at once to celebrate the funeral and, by force, take over the estate?

Two conferences held during the war, the one at Zimmerwald in 1915, the other at Kienthal in 1916, explain the growth of divergence between the two camps of socialism. At Zimmerwald the main emphasis is upon the horrors of war. The need for peace is proclaimed. The socialists who have joined belligerent governments are denounced; a demand is made for peace without annexations or indemnities; and the duty of justly recognising national rights is insisted upon. Save for a phrase which calls upon the proletariat of the world to unite on action (what action is not specified) on behalf of socialism, the resolutions at Zimmerwald might well have come from any congress of pacifists. But at Kienthal, where Lenin was one of the outstanding figures, the atmosphere takes on a different hue. There cannot, it is asserted, be any durable peace under capitalism. The only way thereto lies through the conquest of political power by the masses, and the ownership of capital by the peoples. This can come only as they struggle with increasing intensity against imperialism and its wars so that the struggle may be transformed into a contest between capitalist and proletariat. The Second International is vigorously denounced, and the whole tone of the conference suggests that a great event or a great leader would swing its members into the full tide of revolutionary ardour.

The great event was the Russian Revolution and the event produced the great leader in Lenin. The revolution, of course, was no sudden or unexpected event; it was based upon a series of great failures and accelerated by the utter incapacity and corruption revealed by the Tsarist government during the war. Beginning, in March of 1917, as the normal constitutional upheaval, its early protagonists made the fatal error of assuming that the war was popular with the Russian people and that a change of system could be conducted coincidently with its continuance. The Bolshevik party, under Lenin's leadership, made no such mistake. With the promise of immediate peace they were able to win over the army and the masses to their side; and November of 1917 saw in power a body of men wedded to Marxian doctrine and trained by long experience in the habits of revolution. At home, they created an iron dictatorship the power of which was maintained less by its own effectiveness than by the folly of the European governments. For the latter, angry at the making of peace by the new Russia, and disturbed at the doctrines which it proceeded to enforce, either themselves engaged in war upon it, or subsidised a series of dubious adventurers prepared, for a consideration, to attempt its overthrow. The result was to transform the dictatorship of a party into the government of a nation. The Russian demand for peace found response among the peoples of Europe; and the refusal of governments to pay attention to the response, even when the socialist parties of England, Italy and Germany voted to go to the Stockholm Conference, was probably the worst error they could have made in attacking the new communistic state. For, thereby, they revealed themselves as imperialistic in outlook; and the revelations of the secret treaties, published by the Bolsheviks on their assumption of power, created a disillusion throughout Western Europe which the idealism of President Wilson did little to mitigate. The Stockholm Conference was, indeed, held without them; but it did more to further cleavage among socialists than to make possible a peace of justice. It decided upon a new International, and when the armistice made possible its summons, it was discovered that reformist and revolutionary socialists had each created their separate organisation. That of the former—the restored Second International—was, in essentials, little more than a pacifist society, aiming at socialism, indeed, but within the accepted categories of law. It existed for resolution and protest; it did not exist for action. That of Moscow—the Third International—was created for, and still exists for, the making of world-revolution. It would have no dealings of any kind with the reformist elements of socialism. Its programme was simply the strategy and ends which were the staple of Bolshevist doctrine. Its control was vigorously centralised in Moscow, and it did not permit its adherents to deviate from the path indicated to them. What it was in its origins, it has in essence remained. Estimates of its authority and influence will differ as widely as opinion upon the wisdom of its tactics. It remains, in any case, as a definite challenge to those who believed that social evolution is possible in the medium of peace.

VI

Those who represent the Bolshevists as a set of unprincipled adventurers in German pay do sorry service to the understanding of the greatest event in history since the Reformation. They represent simply that section of the revolutionary party which has adopted the Marxian principles in their most extreme form; their name simply expresses the fact that at a conference held in Brussels and London in 1903, their views won the assent of the majority of the delegates there. Most of their leaders, and notably Lenin and Trotsky, were old and tried revolutionaries, who had served long terms of imprisonment under the Tsarist régime, and had dedicated their lives to the service of their cause. Their methods may have been tyrannical; the price of their success may have been enormous. But it is illegitimate to question either their honesty or their idealism. They were victorious over their opponents for a number of obvious reasons. They were, at the moment of their triumph, the one party in Russia who knew what they wanted and had the iron determination necessary to secure it. They were, also, the one party who were not prepared to compromise with any revolutionary effort which, like that of the first Revolution of March 1917, was merely political in character. They were, further, the only party prepared to buy the support of the masses by making peace at any price at which it could be purchased. The Russian people had ceased to be interested in the war because they were weary of it; the Bolsheviks had never been favourable to the war because they regarded it as simply an imperialist adventure. When to all this is added the fact that their opponents had neither a determined policy nor an efficient machinery, it is not difficult to understand their success in a country so little accustomed as Russia to political habits. And whatever chances there were of their subsequent failure were entirely negatived by the attempts of the Allies to overthrow them. For there was thus aroused on their behalf that same profound patriotism of the Russian people which had displayed itself during the Napoleonic invasion of 1812. Civil war and foreign invasion gave to the Bolsheviks exactly the breathing space they required to measure their position and to revise their mistakes. As the weakness of their Russian opponents was the chief cause of their victory, so the error of their foreign opponents was the chief cause of its consolidation.

It is in any case difficult, and in a short space it is impossible, to assess the achievement of the Bolshevists since they first came into power. On their own confession, they have made innumerable mistakes; but it is probably a sign of their political strength that they have been able to admit them. They sought, in the beginning, to take rapid and gigantic strides towards the general socialisation of the means of production. Factories, workshops, land, the distributive process, were all of them nationalised in wholesale fashion. The expert was, if not dispensed with, at least treated with contempt; and the common man, provided that he sympathised with the Revolution, was dressed in his little brief hour of authority. A dictatorship was established, and opposition of every kind, even from socialist sources, was suppressed with what, to the outsider, seems savage cruelty. Religion was everywhere attacked; education became merely a training in communist ideas; election to the various assemblies were manipulated with a brutal directness that must have caused pangs of envy to the most powerful of American "bosses." The aristocracy and the bourgeoisie, by the mere fact of their origins, were treated as though they embodied original sin. Save thought itself, nothing was outside the sphere of communist dictatorship; and it must be added that the discipline imposed by the party on others was perhaps less strict than that imposed upon its members. The task, it is only fair to say, was overwhelming. The war had left Russia disorganised; civil war and plague and famine made it a shambles. No party could have wrought order from this chaos without methods that savoured of something akin to terrorism.

The central mistake in Bolshevist policy was, it is probable, greatly to underestimate the psychic resistance they would encounter. The outstanding result of their effort has been the abolition of agrarian feudalism in Russia; the peasant has become *de facto* owner of the soil. Herein Russian agrarian life shares all the characteristic features of the new peasant states of Eastern Europe; and there is no special reason to suppose that the Russian village will prove more amenable to communist ideas than the peasantry of other lands. Private trading, moreover, has, though after a bitter struggle, been restored upon something approaching its pre-war scale; and the needs of production have led to the re-introduction of what would elsewhere be described as bourgeois small industry. The idea of equal wages, of which much was made in 1918, has gone; and piecework and the bonus upon output have been glorified in a way that conveys almost an American enthusiasm for such ideas. The large industries have been organised into great trusts, and they resemble, in their working and relation to the State, nothing so much as the railway companies of England and America. Small factories are leased either to their former owners, or to other persons; and their organisation and conduct is not noticeably different from those of other countries. After a disastrous attempt to abolish a money-economy, the normal currency has been restored; and with it has come the usual habits of a State concerned to tax that its budget may be balanced.

Certain special features remain. The State holds the monopoly of foreign trade; and its complete control of the banking system places all credit facilities at its disposal. The Supreme Council of People's Economy, moreover, has its hands upon the flow of production; and since the great trusts are run by boards that it appoints, it may be said to have, and to exercise, final powers of intervention and management in the most important parts of commercial activity. The trade unions, moreover, have nothing of that freedom of action characteristic of England or France; they are rigorously disciplined and may, on an English analogy, be said to live under the shadow of a drastic and permanent Emergency Powers Act. Broadly speaking, there would not be much disagreement with the view that after a premature attempt at communism, the Bolshevists have re-introduced some of the normal features of a capitalist economy, limited, however, by vigorous State control. They hope, it need not be said, that this reaction is merely a transition-stage; for as education in communist principles, particularly among the youth of Russia, becomes general, the movement forward may be facilitated. This is, it may be suggested, a special problem in time; for Russia remains a nation of peasants, and the latter are, very largely, their own economic masters. It is difficult to see how they can avoid an attempt to consolidate their position in the villages by insisting upon a full share in political power. If this occurs, the movement towards a general communism is likely to be slow in coming.

Yet there are certain psychological gains which must not be denied. It is, on any rational view, an immense merit to have got finally rid of the apparatus of Tsarism. A new and more powerful tyranny may have taken its place; but it is at least a tyranny conceived in the interests of the masses. There are, moreover, signs that this is realised in Russia. Observers worthy of credit report a sense of moral stature in the multitude which is a new fact in Russian history. There is a change, too, in the character of the people. "One need only spend a few hours in Moscow," writes Mr. Farbman, "to realise how the events of the last seven years have infected the people with a new fever of activity, self-assertion, and acquisitiveness. Of the notorious dreamy and idle Slav temperament, nothing now remains in Russia." Despite all that has occurred, there seem to have emerged new impulses of hope and energy among the masses. There is widespread poverty and suffering. There is nothing of democracy or liberty in the senses in which those words are understood in Western Europe. But there is a new hope of achievement unknown in previous Russian history; and that hope has kindled a spark of ambition in the proletariat of the West which sets the temper of democratic effort there as the French Revolution did one hundred and thirty years ago.

It is yet difficult not to feel that these results are less the consequence of Bolshevism than of the Bolshevists. They are, as a party, comparable to nothing so much as the Society of Jesus. There is, in both, the same rigorous and unyielding set of dogmas, the same iron rigour of discipline, the same passionate loyalty capable of unlimited self-confidence. The Jesuit who set out to preach his faith in China or the unknown Arctic North-West is not dissimilar to the Communist who volunteers to bury the infected corpses in the cholera epidemic. Like the Jesuit, the Communist has no personal end to secure; he feels himself essentially the servant of a great idea. Like the Jesuit, also, the Russian Communist has the assurance that he works for a cause that is bound in the end to triumph. No one can read the literature of Bolshevism without the sense that its doctrine of predestination is one of the secrets of its success; no one fights so well as the man who has assurance of his ultimate triumph. That certainty produces in its possessors the temperament of the fanatic. They know so surely the rightness of their end that they feel morally entitled to use all means for its accomplishment.

It is this assurance that they have the truth (and, with it, the future) on their side which makes the Bolsheviks so impatient of, and so intolerant to, criticism and dissent. Like all the great spiritual fanatics of history, they cannot help but equate disagreement with sin. The followers of Mahomet, the Ironsides of Cromwell, the Calvinists at Geneva, had the same sublime self-confidence and audacity. Like the Inquisitor in Mr. Shaw's *Saint Joan*, they regret the duty of persecution; but they have no shred of doubt of its absolute necessity. Mistakes are capable of pardon, but not intellectual error, since the truth is there if men will only make the effort to perceive it. Any body of men with kindred ideas will be driven to sacrifice democracy and toleration to a creed that possesses a dictatorship to enforce it.

This, it should be added, is said by way of explanation and not of apology. Anyone who deals with modern communism is dealing with a new religion which has to win its spurs;

and all new religions in that position, as Christianity itself has demonstrated, will use the sword for their propagation. It is this fact which makes the life of Marx the turning-point in communist history. Before his time, its theories were not a programme but a series of moral aphorisms. Marx supplied it with a strategy, and Lenin and his disciples have turned that strategy into an applied philosophy. Nothing is gained by dismissing it either as intellectual or moral error. For, in the first place, no philosophy ever gains a hold upon the minds of men without being a response to aspirations not otherwise satisfied; and, in the second, most great errors in social theory turn out, upon critical examination, to contain at least an index to important truth.

One other remark may be made. The study of the essential principles of communism has a special value because it compels us to submit more orthodox doctrines to a closer examination than they are wont to receive. It is a warning to us not to confound, as Tocqueville put it, the institutions to which we are accustomed with the necessary foundations of society. Englishmen especially, with over six hundred years of parliamentary institutions behind them, are accustomed to think of representative democracy as the ideal pattern towards which the progressive State inevitably moves. Yet representative democracy is, in the world as a whole, confined to a very small portion of its surface; and the sceptic might reasonably interject the observation that we are witnessing its increasing rejection rather than its increasing acceptance. Nor is that all. Many who have been horrified at the price paid for the establishment of Bolshevism in Russia have sometimes welcomed, and not seldom condoned, the dictatorships of Italy and Hungary, the methods of which have been remarkably similar in substance. The classic purposes of the State, liberty, equality, the career open to the talents, social justice, accordingly need examination not merely in terms of their virtue as ends, but in terms of their practicability as ends in the light of the institutions through which they are to be achieved. Communism does not deny those ends as good. But it denies absolutely and with passion that they have meaning in terms of the modern State. It brings to that denial a completely alternative view both of the meaning of historic phenomena, and of the methods by which, as ends, they be achieved. No one who seriously acquaints himself with that alternative but must be impressed by its power. For even if, upon analysis, it be rejected, it compels the adjustment of one's own philosophy to a richer and wider perspective. It emphasises neglected aspects of history and, by the authority of its emphasis, translates them into demands. The future will either secure their satisfaction or submit to its control.

CHAPTER II

THE MATERIALIST INTERPRETATION OF HISTORY

I

EVERY theory of social action is ultimately a philosophy of history. It attempts, as best it may, to read in the experience of mankind the lessons which would justify its own special urgency. With Bossuet, and, in a sense, with Vico, that lesson is the dominion of Providence over the effort of mankind; with Fichte, it is the victory of reason, of free inquiry, over the blind demands of faith; with Bonald and de Maistre it is the necessity of religion as the one power able to compel that subordination without which men are the necessary victims of anarchic disorder.

Marx is no exception to the general rule. While his own interpretation is not, in its large outlines, original, the peculiar emphasis and direction he gave to it are all his own. To understand it, indeed, it is necessary to consider its meaning in the light of Hegel's work; for Marx was, in a special sense, the pupil of Hegel, even though the turn he gave to the master's doctrine was one which the latter would doubtless have been the first to repudiate. For Hegel, any adequate philosophy of history must be based upon the idea of evolution. He insists that the world of human experience is created by reason; and because reason is a principle of growth, its embodiment in the facts is meaningless save as we study it in the terms of development. History, then, for him, becomes the slow development of the idea of freedom; and institutions are the efforts of men to embody that idea in concrete externality. Institutions, in fact, are the idea; without them it can have no meaning. Each age in history records an idea of justice which represents the effort or capacity of that age to realise its substance. But its understanding is necessarily partial and imperfect; and as the logical consequence of its limitation becomes apparent, the contradiction between idea and need becomes obvious. The result is a new form of the idea, based upon the negation of its predecessor. The negation, indeed, is constructive. It possesses a positive character merely because it supplies something wanting in what has gone before. It does not destroy; rather it mitigates or fulfils by compelling a new combination of the elements it has inherited.

Being, therefore, is becoming; each element of life, in the process called by Hegel dialectic, is in continuous transition to new form. And in the variety we encounter, each element is always accompanied by its antithesis. Love involves hate, good evil, freedom slavery. Every idea contains these positive and negative elements; though the negative, by its correction of inadequacy, has a positive character also. Progress—which, for Hegel, is the movement towards perfect freedom—is thus the contradiction of one aspect by the other. Each is essential to, and comes to be by reason of, its opponent. Without feudalism, there could not have been the middle-class State; without the middle-class State, there could not have been a proletarian movement. The working out of the idea of private property is necessarily a revelation of its imperfections; and the remedy for these is supplied by the antithesis of common ownership. There comes, that is to say, a stage in the history of the idea when its utility for its age draws near completion; its antithesis then begins the work of creative destruction, only to be destroyed in its own turn as its purpose is fulfilled.

With Hegel, of course, the doctrine became a philosophy of conservatism. It enabled him, not altogether logically, to reject both liberalism and representative institutions, and to find in the absolute Prussian State the highest embodiment of freedom as a universal idea. What, however, interested Marx in

Hegel was not the result but the method. It was the notion of each age producing the corrective to its own error that threw light, for him, upon his own problems. Nor was insight wanting in many of Hegel's own *obiter dicta.* His insistence, for example, that the philosophy of an age merely expresses its view of what it needs; his perception that the centralised State cannot develop until the people are divided into rich and poor; his view of Greek colonisation, and his emphasis upon the geographical factor of history; his conception, in a word, of ideas as a function of a given material environment gave to Marx the clue he required. As Feuerbach and Strauss applied the Hegelian dialectic to the destruction of Christianity, so Marx applied it to the destruction of capitalism. He was the first to see the significance of the method as a factor in social analysis; and no one can doubt the power of the lever in his hands.

Like all great conceptions, the notion of the materialistic interpretation of history is essentially simple in character. It is simply the insistence that the material conditions of life, taken as a whole, primarily determine the changes in human thought. It is not some indwelling idea, Providence, the World-Spirit, or Natural Reason, which secures the changes that occur. These are conceptions invented by men, and interpreted by men, in their effort to explain the character of the world about them. The colour and connotation of our ideas is always given by, and shaped from, the manner in which men have to gain the means of life.

Were the conception to be left there, it would not be of great importance. For it would simply insist that man's ideas are born of his experience, which is an obvious platitude. But Marx went on to assert that, within the framework of the general environment, the vital characteristic, the category which is above all important, is the system of production which obtains at a given time. The productive forces of society are those which, personal and impersonal, enable men to satisfy their needs. They bring into being, at each state of their interaction, institutions and ideas which, in their turn, react upon them. Law, religion, the forms of government, the place of men in their various social groupings, all these are primarily determined by the system of production which obtains. Translated into abstractions, they become moral, political, and religious systems, which simply represent the ideas of men about the worth, in some given aspect, of the system under which they live. The groundwork of each generation is the way in which it produces the means of life. Thereon, and thereon only, is erected the system of institutions and ideas which represent their reflection upon their meaning and value. " Men make their own history," said Marx, " but they do not do so spontaneously under conditions they have themselves chosen. On the contrary, they must make it upon terms already handed down to them and determined." They are, briefly speaking, a function of the way in which they satisfy their wants. That is the key to social evolution.

Economic necessity is therefore the foundation upon which all other parts of the social structure must be built. In the *Communist Manifesto* Marx attempted to summarise his view of historic development in terms of this view. Nor is it possible to deny its truth. It is clear, for instance, that feudal society transforms all institutions to suit its special needs. Law is built in terms of relationships which fix men into a landholding system conceived in the interests of its possessors; even religion adapts itself to the needs of feudalism. The church which begins as the prophet of equality has no difficulty in adjusting its doctrines to the social hierarchy which feudalism requires. As mediæval society declines, there grows into its place the middle-class State, with its emphasis upon private property. Little by little it sweeps away ideas and institutions which serve the mediæval notion of status to replace them by others built upon the conception of contract. The individual replaces the corporation; Protestantism, with its emphasis upon the individual and his conscience, replaces Rome. The petty sovereignties of feudalism give way before the national State with its facilitation of commerce by the promotion of order and legal simplicity. When the despotic monarchies of the *ancien régime* hinder this development, they, too, are destroyed by the necessity of yielding to its claims. At each stage of the historic process we encounter not abstract notions with an independent life, but concrete necessities set by a material environment which makes them inevitable.

So Marx would explain a given set of historic ideas. Not less important is his view of how they come to change. Material conditions do not stand still. New markets, new methods, and new raw materials are discovered; organisation, whether of production or distribution, is improved; and the economic system becoming obsolete, a change in its foundations becomes essential. But its essentials are the whole structure of society, its ranks and classes, its laws and form of State, its religious institutions and intellectual systems. There is a contradiction between the existing theory of society and its external environment. Men have to learn to think in the new terms that environment requires.

Mr. Bertrand Russell has given us a very happy illustration of this relationship between thought and the material world. The case for the emancipation of women, as he points out,[1] is as old as Plato; the arguments on its behalf were urged with irresistible force by thinkers like Mary Wollstonecraft and John Stuart Mill. Yet, despite this cogency, they were broadly impotent until the entrance of women into industry was so widespread, that a readjustment of their political position became inevitable. Not less significant is the history, between the Reformation and the Revolution of 1688, of the doctrine of toleration. Scattered thinkers like Robert Brown, statesmen like William of Orange, were able to see its value; but to their own day it was a plea without either moral or intellectual validity. But when, in the seventeenth century, it was found incompatible with commercial prosperity to persecute, men had no difficulty in affirming that a religion of love was incompatible with repression made in its name. Ideas, doubtless, always lag behind the environment of which they are a part; but sooner or later their adjustment is effected with an ease which makes men wonder at their previous conservatism.

There is, moreover, another aspect to the picture. New truths are born of new environments, and they have, as we have seen, to fight their way painfully to acceptance. In every social order a division of men may be made into those who are on the side of the existing position, and those who seek to change

[1] *Bolshevism in Theory and Practice*, p. 122.

it. In general, that division is between the possessing class in a given society and those dependent upon it. To the former belongs the authority of government. They utilise their power to make the laws and to operate the institutions in the interest of their class. They identify social good with their own preservation. Attacks upon them they will punish as sedition. Education, justice, religious teaching, are tempered to serve their interests. This is not, it should be insisted, a conscious effort on their part to exclude members of the non-possessing class from a share in social benefit; it is simply the natural reaction to the material environment. But the class excluded from the privileges of possession naturally, also, desires a share in them. Hence arises, in every society, a struggle between classes for its control. Sometimes, compromise is possible because the system represented by the possessing class has not yet reached the limit of its utility; then we get concessions from above which often bring with them a period of comparative tranquillity. But when the system has reached its apogee, compromise becomes impossible. No margin is left within which the possessing class can at once concede, in any serious way, and yet maintain its supremacy. Then revolution, as in England in 1642, or France in 1789, supervenes forcibly to alter the character of the State. A new balance of power is created, and institutions are adjusted to the new synthesis.

As soon, then, as private property became the outstanding feature of Western civilisation, institutional change became a function of class antagonism. All history is full of the record of this struggle; most of the great legislators of antiquity, Lycurgus and Solon, for example, were men seeking to mitigate its acerbity. Patrician and plebeian in Rome, feudal lord and serf in mediæval Europe, squirearchy and bourgeoisie in the Industrial Revolution, capitalist and wage-earner in our own day, the struggle between these contending forces for the mastery of the State represents the universal antithesis everywhere discoverable. It determines the social ideas of each epoch. "What else," wrote Marx, in the *Communist Manifesto*, "does the history of ideas demonstrate except that intellectual production changes its character in proportion with the changes in material production. The governing ideas of each period are always the ideas of its governing class." New theories, in fact, are nothing other than the expression of new social forces detected in the material environment by some thinker more prescient than the rest; and they gain in authority in the degree that this environment makes them increasingly the expression of its ideas. "When the ancient world was at its last gasp," declares the

Communist Manifesto, "the ancient religions were overthrown by Christianity. When Christian ideas succumbed in the eighteenth century to rationalism, feudal society fought its death-battle with the then revolutionary bourgeoisie. The doctrines of religious freedom and liberty of conscience simply gave expression to the rule of free competition within the domain of knowledge."

II

This view of history, it should be emphasised, is not a communist discovery. Historical materialism is as old as Aristotle; and thinkers like Harrington and Madison have made it the corner-stone of their systems. Nor did communism originate the theory of class-antagonism as the motive power of change. So far from being, as Engels asserted, "the unique and exclusive property of Marx," it is characteristic of almost every radical doctrinaire after the French Revolution. It is set out with emphasis in Babeuf's *Manifeste des Egaux* (1796),[1] a document which, not unsignificantly, is not referred to by Marx in his discussion of the Utopian socialists. It was asserted by Blanqui in the trial of 1832 where the Society of the Friends of the

[1] Babeuf, indeed, may well claim to be the founder of the idea of proletarian dictatorship.

People was condemned by the government of Louis-Philippe. It was a commonplace with Saint-Simon and his disciples; Bazard, very notably, in the *Doctrine Saint-simonienne*, speaks of "men divided into two classes, the exploiters and exploited, masters and slaves." So, also, German socialism, as with Karl Grün, as early as 1844, wrote of history as "no more than a continuous war, in essence, between the fortunate, the possessors, the conquerors, against the unhappy, the disinherited, the oppressed;" and he inquires whether history can secure a classless society. And among non-socialist thinkers, Linguet in the middle eighteenth century, and Sismondi in the early nineteenth, had held similar views. One neglected French thinker, Constantine Pecquer, may be said to have outlined the theory of historic materialism with a clarity as great, and a conviction as intense, as Marx himself ever displayed.

Marx, indeed, may be said, if a little grudgingly, to have recognised this. "The founders of these systems," he says of the Utopian Socialists in the *Communist Manifesto*, "see the class antagonisms, as well as the action of the decomposing elements in the prevailing form of society." Where he, in particular, and communists in general, differ from their forerunners is in the deductions made from the general theorem. For while the earlier thinkers, as a rule, seek some basis of stability in a non-economic idea of justice, as with Sismondi, or in some special pattern of institutions, as with Saint-Simon, Fourier and Proudhon, Marx takes his stand on quite different grounds. He insists, and his followers insist even more vigorously, that the transition from one system of production to another is necessarily marked by violent revolution; and he argues that the conflict between bourgeoisie and proletariat is the final phase of the class-struggle. These differences are fundamental in texture. From the one derives the whole formidable apparatus of political method and strategy that distinguishes the communist from his opponent; from the other is born the sense of ultimate optimism which characterises communism. It is self-confident and audacious because it has been taught that the inevitabilities of the future are upon its side.

Class-antagonism, we have seen, is the instrument which forces social theories and institutions into closer harmony with the system of production. What are the marks by which a class can be known? Men, clearly enough, may be divided by colour, or religion, or political allegiance; they may be grouped as freemasons or clericals, as nominalists or realists. On the Marxian view, the scientifically valid method of classifying them is by the way in which they earn their living. On this view, modern society is divisible into two great groups, the capitalist and the wage-earner. Of the one, the outstanding feature is the fact that he lives by owning; he has land, or shares, or workshops, or access to raw material; of the other, the dominating fact is that they live by, and are mainly dependent upon, wages. Marx is not concerned with minor features of distinction. Some wage-earners may have investments; many of the working-class to-day have holdings in co-operative societies. Most capitalists either manage, or assist in managing, the properties with which they are connected. Marx does not deny the possibility of minor sub-divisions along these lines. They are, for him, as insignificant as the fact that among capitalists some are successful and others unsuccessful, while some wage-earners are well-paid while their fellows are compelled to live upon the very margin of subsistence. His essential point is the insistence that however the two great classes are sub-divided, one is united with itself by the fact that it lives by the sale of its labour, and the other by the fact that it owns, in its capital, the means of production.

That difference, for the communist, is fundamental. It means that between the two classes there is a permanent and ultimately irreconcilable hostility. There may be periods of greater or less tension between them; but, in the last resort, one of them can live only by the conquest of the other. For the wage-earners, as a class, are concerned only with securing the highest possible price for their labour, while the capitalists, again as a class, are constrained, in the interest of profits, to purchase it at the minimum price. In the contest between buyer and seller of labour, an antagonism is involved the nature of which touches the foundations of the State. Labour, it is clear, must either find a purchaser quickly, or starve; capital is subject to no such disability. Their relationship, therefore, by definition places a weapon of oppression and exploitation in the hands of the capitalist, and this can only be removed as the relationship itself is destroyed. But to destroy that relationship is to destroy the private ownership of capital, which means in effect its social ownership. This, in its turn, means a society without masters or men; and the destruction, accordingly, of this division is the final social struggle in that it produces a classless society.

It is in the detailed discussion of the means whereby this change is effected that the peculiar Marxian doctrine is revealed. "Middle-class historians," wrote Marx in 1852, "long ago described the evolution of class-struggles, and political economists explained the economic physiology of classes. My contribution has been to add the following theses: (1) that the existing classes are bound up with certain phases of material production; (2) that the class-struggle necessarily leads to the dictatorship of the proletariat; (3) that this dictatorship is merely the transition to the abolition of all classes, and the creation of a free and equal society." The proof of these theses is built partly on the grounds of historic fact, and partly on prophetic deduction from them. The necessary hostility between capital and labour leads to the formation of trade unions. These, in their early stages, foreshadow the coming of the struggle between bourgeoisie and proletariat. For the experience of trade unions slowly but inevitably convinces the workers that so long as capitalism persists, their subjection as a class is a necessary phase of the social order. They begin to see that its overthrow, the attainment, that is, of the common ownership of the means of production, is the condition precedent to their release. In growing numbers, therefore, they begin to see that their task is the preparation of this class-struggle. Their hostility to their masters becomes infused with a general idea; they think as communists. They prepare consciously for their emancipation. But Marx insists that, for the completion of the process, the emancipation must be attained by the workers themselves. They must not be satisfied with reforms, nor put their trust, from a lack of audacity or self-confidence, in the sense of justice displayed by bourgeois thinkers and politicians who are appalled at the existence of misery and want. They must seek, not the mitigation, but the exacerbation of the class-struggle.

For any concessions that are won from capitalism are evidence merely of its weakness. They do not prevent the inevitability of a final conflict between the capitalist and the wage-earner. Things like the battle over rates of wages, or the length of the working-day are, so to speak, merely an index to the greater struggle beyond. The workers' task is not to aid their masters in finding terms upon which capitalism may endure, but to discover the period at which its overthrow may be successfully prepared. To that end they must capture the machinery of the State; since it is through its possession of this machinery that the governing class enforces its will. And, possessing it, the workers must then utilise its authority to transform a capitalist into a communist society.

The trade unions, then, awaken the class-consciousness of the masses, and direct their effective energies to the capture of the political State. Upon the basis they provide, a Labour Party is built up which becomes the expression in the political sphere, of the class-consciousness typified by them in the economic sphere. The Labour Party's function is to be the class-conscious vanguard of the advancing proletariat. It will, under favourable conditions, find circumstances not unhelpful to its task. There will be a more or less complete political democracy, and this can be turned to communist advantage. Not, indeed, that the democracy so established is ever real. "This democracy," wrote Lenin, "is always bound by the narrow framework of capitalist exploitation, and consequently always remains, in reality, a democracy only for the minority, only for the possessing classes, only for the rich. Freedom in capitalist society always remains more or less the same as it was in the ancient Greek republics, that is, freedom for the slave-owners. The modern wage-slaves, in virtue of capitalist exploitation, remain to such an extent crushed by want and poverty that they 'cannot be bothered with democracy,' have 'no time for politics'; and, in the ordinary peaceful course of events, the majority of the population is debarred from participating in public political life."

In the communist view, therefore, capitalist democracy is hypocritical for two reasons. It is, firstly, narrowly political; the absence of democracy in the economic sphere means the virtual exclusion of the toiling millions from any share in it. Because capitalism makes them slaves, they have the mentality of slaves. And, secondly, it is democratic only to the point that the foundations of capitalism are not threatened. Let the workers, for instance, obtain a majority at the polls, and seek to effect a transformation to communism by peaceful means, and they will find that the capitalist class will seek their violent overthrow. Ordinary political effort, therefore, is only of value as a demonstration to the workers of the futility of peace. It does not postpone the conflict that must come.

And for the communist that conflict is definite war, with the methods and instruments of war; the formulæ of peace are out of place until the victory of the proletariat is complete. How exactly the conflict will come, it is not possible to state dogmatically. Marx himself predicted that it would arrive first in the most advanced industrial countries; a prophecy which the experience of Russia has contradicted. He believed that, as a rule, it would grow out of a revolution in which, with the aid of the revolutionary working-class, a democracy of social reformers would come into power. The duty of the communist was then plain; he must separate from the new régime and fight it, as Lenin compelled his followers to do after the first Russian Revolution. He must seek to weaken the new government at every turn so as to facilitate his own access to power. "The workers," Marx told the League of Communists in 1850, ". . . must aim at preventing the subsidence of the revolutionary excitement immediately after the victory. . . . During and after the struggle, they must seize every opportunity to present their own demands side by side with those of the middle-class democrats. . . . Guarantees must be exacted, and the new rulers must be compelled to make every possible promise and concession, which is the surest way to compromise them." From this position to definite armed revolution is only a step. Once the communist is in power, "progressive development," as Lenin says, "marches through the dictatorship of the proletariat. It cannot do otherwise, for there is no one else who can *break the resistance* of the exploiting capitalist, and no other way of doing it." The more thoroughgoing, indeed, that dictatorship is, the shorter will be the period of transition to communism; for weakness here provokes counter-revolution which defers the effective abolition of private property in the means of production.

We shall discuss elsewhere in this book the theory of a dictatorship and its significance; here, to complete the picture, something may be said of the communist view of society after the revolution is complete, and its outlook upon the relation of class-structure to national and international organisation. Upon the first problem communists have been studiously, and with justice, vague; for a new system of production is bound to create ideas that it is impossible to foresee in any detail. All that can be done is to posit certain basic principles.

The subjection dependent upon the present division of labour will disappear; there will be no opposition between brain and manual work. Labour will cease to be a commodity, bought and sold in order to achieve the bare means of subsistence. The State will wither away because, in Lenin's phrase, "when people have become accustomed to observe the fundamental principles of social life, and their labour is so productive, they will voluntarily work *according to their abilities*." Men will overpass what Marx termed "the narrow horizon of bourgeois law." "Society," says the *Communist Manifesto*, "will be able to inscribe upon its banner: From each according to his powers; to each according to his needs." And we are warned by Lenin that sneers at his view as Utopian are out of place. "The *anticipation*," he says, "of the great socialists that it *will* arrive, assumes neither the present productive powers of labour, *nor the present* unthinking man in the street, capable of spoiling, without reflection, the stores of social wealth, and of demanding the impossible." There will, in fact, be a different human nature, or, at least, a human nature which expresses itself in different wants from the present; it is perhaps because of this that Bukharin insists so strongly that "the monopoly of education must become the privilege of the proletariat, if the proletariat is to win."

The communist is clear that the victory of

his movement is dependent upon the occurrence of a world-revolution. "The realisation of proletarian dictatorship," writes Bukharin, "is gravely imperilled in one country unless active assistance is given by the workers of other lands." Marx himself never denied the reality of nationalism, though for him, as for his successors, its hold upon the workers was a part of the defences of capitalism. The communist admits that love of country is real and widespread. But he insists also that it must be overcome. The worker's real country is his class. Under capitalism, the workers have no real share in power. The political institutions of their country are merely a means for their exploitation. Since their task is to destroy the bourgeois State, to defend it, as in the late war, is to be false to their historic mission. It is to suggest that they have interests in common with their oppressors. But, in fact, they can only have a country by seizing the State, and they can only seize the State for communist ends successfully, by uniting with the working-classes of other countries. Nor must the worker be led away by pacifist ideals. Disarmament is impossible for the capitalist State since, of necessity, it lives by war to secure markets and raw materials from its rivals. The worker, therefore, who supports pacifist effort, simply prevents those whom he influences from service to the armed struggle for communism. So long as the class-struggle remains unresolved, to yield to nationalist feeling is to betray, therefore, the highest allegiance the worker can know. The only significance of the worker's country to him is the fact that it happens to be his immediate battlefield in the coming conflict. Moral appeal it can have none until its capitalist government has been overthrown.

III

It is worth while to insist upon what the materialist interpretation of history is not, before discussing its general validity. It has no necessary connection, in the first place, with the metaphysical theory of materialism. That doctrine, though communists in general adopt it, is equally compatible with Buckle's view that climate is the decisive factor in historic events. Nor does it insist that economic conditions are the sole cause of change; it merely argues that they are its main cause. Roughly speaking, it is an argument to the effect that man's situation is the preceptor of his duty, and that in that situation economic elements are paramount simply because the means of life are the first thing to which men must pay attention.

In this simple form, it is impossible not to regard the theory as in the main true. It is clear, for example, that the substance of legal categories is largely determined by their economic context. Contract, tort, the law of husband and wife, are all of them set and altered by the system of production out of which they grow. More specifically, a rule like the " common employment " doctrine in English law [1] could only have been born in a capitalist society; and the limitations upon the suability of the State in contract all bear upon them the marks of a business civilisation. The adjustment, moreover, of church practice to its economic environment has been very striking; the way, for example, in which the doctrine of grace received an interpretation which made business success a proof of God's favour, and poverty an index to His anger, is proof that ecclesiastical theory does not evade the general ambit of the doctrine. And anyone who considers the history of the interpretation of the American Constitution will find little difficulty in seeing in its attitude to problems like those of child labour, or the State regulation of wages and hours, a proof of the general truth of the materialist view. There is no department of human life in which the governing ideas and institutions will not be found, upon examination, to be largely a reflection of a given set of economic conditions.

[1] Cf. Webb, *History of Trade Unionism* (ed. of 1920), pp. 364–6.

We must be careful, indeed, not to push the theory too far. There are particular sets of facts in which it is not helpful as an explanation; and there are others where the obvious requirements of an economic environment cannot be met through the pressure of non-economic factors. They will not wholly explain, even though they are often relevant to, the actions of an individual; as Lassalle, for example, or Robert Owen. Often enough, a man's political creed is born, not of an economic situation, but of an intense psychological dislike for the atmosphere of his family. Nor can either religious or nationalist movements be wholly explained in religious terms. The loyalty of Catholic working-men to their religion, the fierce separatism of the Balkans, both involve methods of explanation which have reference to a human nature not exclusively determined by material conditions. Possibly the Catholic working-man is unwise in preferring his Church to his class; and certainly the nationalism of the Balkans, with its perpetual recurrence of war, is the chief cause of its economic backwardness. But, in cases like these, the rational interest of men is overcome by distracting counter-currents of loyalty which afford them satisfaction superior to that which reason might afford.

Here, indeed, it may be argued, is the real weakness of materialism as a philosophy of history. It is too exclusively preoccupied with a rational theory of human action to remember how much of man's effort is non-rational in character. " The larger events in the political life of the world," writes Mr. Bertrand Russell, " are determined by the interaction of material conditions and human passions." Obviously the latter can be modified in their operation by intelligence; but obviously, also, the modification is at best but partial. When we estimate, therefore, the character of a social system we must measure not merely the effect upon men of the way in which they earn their bread, but of the wider total effect upon them of the chance in that system to satisfy their chief impulses. Men may choose a less advantageous economic order, even when its utility is obviously exhausted, because they prefer its psychological results to those of its antithesis. A state, for example, which did not afford adequate opportunity to energetic and determined men would rapidly change even if it satisfied the inert majority of its members.

All this, however, is merely a footnote to the general truth of the materialist interpretation; it does not destroy its general adequacy. The difficulties emerge less in this aspect than when we come to its communist application. Here, critics have naturally fastened upon two things. They deny the validity of class-antagonism as a permanent social fact; and they argue that there is no reason to accept the Marxian deductions therefrom as an accurate prevision of the future.

We are not for the moment concerned with the political or ethical results of the doctrine of class-war; that must be a matter for discussion in later chapters. What is here important is the question whether it is true. Those who deny it usually do so upon two grounds. They argue, first, that there is an interdependence of social interests which makes it impossible for one class to be injured without all being injured; and, secondly, they argue that, in each social conflict that arises there is an objectively just solution which is the good of the community as a whole. A minor argument is sometimes employed to the effect that the class-consciousness of which Marx speaks is either non-existent or confined to an insignificant minority of society.

In fact, however, none of these views really touches the core of the communist position. The Marxian does not deny the interdependence of classes: what he insists upon is that in the relationship of this interdependence the interests of the capitalist class are considered superior to those of the working-class. It would certainly be difficult for any observer to urge with seriousness that this is not the case. Rarely, indeed, in history does a party or class in power deliberately sacrifice its own well-being to that of others. The history of things like the franchise, education, the administration of justice, the laws of inheritance, of, that is to say, privilege in general, is not the history of its voluntary surrender by its possessors; every concession won has been secured only after hard fighting, in which, very often, either the threat or fact of violence has been an integral part of the victory. "Had the people of England," said Mr. Gladstone, "obeyed the precept to eschew violence and maintain order, the liberties of this country would never have been obtained." The communist answer to a theory of social interdependence is an admission of its truth and an argument that, under the present scheme, its benefits are not justly divided between classes. This seems well within the facts.

Nor is the second argument much more tenable. It is true that in most social conflicts the parties demand more than they feel they ought to have, and that each is but little careful of the well-being of those indirectly affected by the dispute. But a theory which urges the existence of an objectively just decision in the dispute omits to declare who is to determine what that decision shall be. The communist, from his standpoint necessarily, denies that any such arbitrator can be found. For into his decision there will enter a stream of ideas and prejudices begotten of the special complex of interests to which he belongs, even if he be unconscious of their presence. Nor can a capitalist government be regarded, in any just sense, as an impartial judge. Its main purpose is, he argues, to uphold capitalism; and that makes it *a priori* inclined to favour one of the disputants. Anyone who examines, for instance, the series of disputes in the British coal industry since 1919 will find it difficult to maintain that the government of the day has acted impartially as between miners and mine owners. Whenever the interests of capitalism have required it, the results of inquiries have been evaded; and even when their tenor has been verbally accepted, care has been taken to deny their spirit in applying them.

To accept the materialist conception is not, of course, to say that it explains all historic phenomena. There are passages in Marx's works in which this claim seems to have been made; and some of his less cautious disciples have written—wrongly—as though this was the view that he took. In fact, Marx was himself, as a rule, insistent upon the limits within which the theory applies; and he was well aware that while productive systems act upon men, men also react upon productive systems. Criticism of the doctrine, indeed, should concentrate less upon its general outline than upon the communist prophecies which have grown out of it. It is difficult, in the first place, to see why the communist should be assured of the ultimate triumph of the proletariat. An observer of modern capitalism might well argue that the evidence points not to some single and universal solution, but to a variety of quite different results. What may occur, for instance, in a small and highly industrialised country like England, may bear little resemblance to the destiny of peasant civilisations like Roumania and Hungary; and the mere problem of size in America might well make the issue there qualitatively different from what it is in most European countries.

Nor is this all. A revolution that failed might easily lead to a Fascist dictatorship which would discover new forms of industrial organisation more nearly resembling feudalism than anything we have known under the régime of free contract. Marx's view, in short, that a given system of production is governed by inevitable "laws" which direct its outcome unduly simplifies the problem. For those "laws" are merely tendencies which are, at each instant of time, subject to a pressure which makes prophecy of their operation at best a hazardous adventure. The currents of fact and thought which the communist emphasises are undoubtedly there; but there are also counter-currents of fact and thought upon which sufficient stress is rarely laid.

It is worth while, here, to remember the

circumstance under which Marx himself wrote. He knew well the two revolutionary periods of 1789 and 1848; his views were largely generalisations built upon them. The insight he displayed in their analysis was remarkable; but it is difficult not to believe that, at times, the agitator in him was victorious over the scientist. His view is obviously built upon a confidence in rationalism which most psychologists would now judge to be excessive. It has in it that optimistic temper which stamps him as the child of the Enlightenment. Tennyson's "far-off divine event towards which the whole creation moves" has just the same serene certainty, Wordsworth's view of evil as the parent of good has the same happy triumph of faith over doubt, as Marx's insistence that, however often defeated, the proletariat emerges triumphant. He writes of a social system as though it were a species that must conform to the morphological tests of the naturalist. It has no function save to unfold the necessary stages of its evolution. But no social system is, in fact, of this kind. Its life is not merely an inevitable unfolding of inherent tendencies. There are always the novel and unexpected to give the lie to our predictions.

But the communist reliance upon a kind of natural law in social evolution leads him seriously to underestimate the power of forces which are of a non-economic kind. The degree to which nationalism, for instance, will resist economic necessity is remarkable. The mysterious nature of herd-impulse may be admitted; but our ignorance of its nature ought not to blind us to its significance. An English working-man ought, doubtless, to feel that he has more in common with the French or German worker than with the English capitalist. The fact remains that, in general, he gives no sign of such feeling. Some would add that Marx underestimated also the power of religion to influence the actions of men; though anyone who measures the substance of Christian doctrine with the achievement of Christian civilisation may well doubt whether, in this realm, Marx went very far astray.

Nor is it easy to see why his view of the communist state should be accepted. If the revolution he foresaw became universal, there is no inherent reason why the result should be the kind of society he desired. For, in the first place, the intensity of destruction now requisite to the overthrow of a social system might well make impossible a society in which generous impulses had opportunity; and, in the second place, while economic classes might, by hypothesis, disappear, another form of class-rule, that of a doctrinal aristocracy, for example, might take its place. The poison of power is notorious, and it is difficult to see why communists should be held immune from its toxins. It is, indeed, so much the most powerful of the factors by which men in politics are moved that there is no theoretical reason why those who make the communist revolution, or their successors, should abdicate from the pleasant task of exercising authority over their fellows. Ideologies produce economic systems, just as economic systems produce ideologies. The communist emphasises the second, but he is too little willing to see the possible consequences of the first.

We cannot, either, overlook the possibilities that better industrial organisation and the prospects of scientific discovery might easily make of capitalism a system able to satisfy the main wants of the workers. It might then be true of them, as it seems to be true of the American worker in our own day, that they would thereby be led to exchange political power for material comfort. Capitalism is not an unchanging phenomenon; and the margin of possible improvement, under its ægis, is larger than its critics like to admit. The intensity of production, for instance, which might follow a general level of high wages, might, so far from leading to revolution, prove a safeguard against it by the great increase it secured in the average standard of life. We may agree with Marx that, unless capitalism proves itself capable of large reforms, it is destined to perish; but that does not commit us to the theory that communism will take its place. For, in the first place, the breakdown of capitalism might result not in communism, but in anarchy from which there might emerge some dictatorship unrelated in principle to communist ideals; or, in the second, the victory of the working-class might lead to the discovery that the operation of a communist system is impossible. Neither Marx nor his disciples, that is to say, can predict of a revolution more than that a change in the system of production will be the precursor of a change in the habits of society. If that change means the social ownership of the means of production, it is possible to assume that the habits of society will be better, since, under the present system, these have but little relation to justice. But the assumption, however justified, still remains an act of faith.

There is, however, a defence for the Marxian view of inevitable revolution that must not be overlooked. Few of the great social changes with which history acquaints us but have been accompanied by violent upheaval; and even the prediction of its inevitability, as in the France of the *ancien régime*, has not moved those in power to make the concessions which might have avoided it. Why, it may be asked, should we assume that in this respect the future will be different from the past?

On any *a priori* ground, we have no reason to make any such assumption. Those who possess to-day the instruments of economic power are certainly not less anxious to preserve them than were their predecessors. We can only argue that the general democratisation of political institutions makes popular want more effective in securing response than at any previous time; and that the cost of revolution, even if unsuccessful, is now so immense that few Governments would be prepared to risk its coming if concession could purchase its avoidance. We can point, also, to the fact that whereas to Marx one of the root causes of revolution was the increasing misery of the working-class, the evidence seems to prove a genuine and important improvement in their condition during the last hundred years. If that condition continues (a condition, however, which involves the maintenance of peace), the resultant prosperity might leave a margin within which changes of the necessary range might be secured.

It is, of course, impossible to say that they will be secured. Modern civilisation is, at best, a fragile thing; and while there are revolutionary forces at work which, in a period of war or similar crisis, might easily make for disaster, there are also counter-revolutionary forces the hostility of which to social change are not less dangerous. Lenin in Russia must be paralleled by Mussolini in Italy. Nor must we make too much of the view that the average worker has little thought of the class-relationship which Marxism postulates. In ordinary times this is true, and Marx himself both admitted and explained it. But revolutions always spring from the acts of a minority, and their power is enormous to educate rapidly into exactly that class-consciousness postulated by communists. The two outstanding facts before us are the inevitability of change, and the certainty that any serious attack upon the position of the workers will meet with resistance. Unless, that is to say, there is a considered and continuous effort after social improvement, their united influence might easily demonstrate the truth of the communist position.

We conclude, then, that the materialist interpretation of history is, as general doctrine, undeniable. In the context of communism, there is no necessary connection between its theses and the inferences and predictions made by Marx. A necessary connection may, however, be made. The only way to avoid its coming is to prove by social policy that it is unnecessary. We cannot urge with any profound conviction that this is being done. The invasion of human demands for the benefit of a few is still the rule rather than the exception in history. The strength of the communist position lies in its insistence that it will remain the rule. Thereby it draws the attention of the disinherited to the glaring disparities of our social order. History shows clearly that they will act upon their observation unless they are shown that they can obtain by other means the reasonable satisfaction of their desires.

CHAPTER III

COMMUNIST ECONOMICS

I

COMMUNIST economics are almost entirely a polemic in defence of Marx's *Capital;* the system laid down by the master has been accepted by his successors with a fierce intensity like that of the Puritan for the Bible or the Mahomedan for the Koran. It has aroused the most bitter of controversies, and its interpretations have been almost as numerous as the men who have sought to explain it. For the Marxians themselves it has, quite naturally, superseded all other systems; to the critics, it is a mass of patent contradictions. Socialists themselves do not always accept it. The German revisionists, led by Bernstein, have insisted that its theses are out of accord with the trend of economic facts. The English Fabians derive their economic theories rather from Mill and Jevons than from their own socialist predecessors. The French Syndicalists regard Marxian economics as of high fighting value, but true only of a world of pure concepts quite different from the world about us. "Marxian socialism," writes Mr. Keynes,[1] "must always remain a portent to the historians of opinion—how a doctrine so illogical and so dull can have exercised so powerful and enduring an influence over the minds of men and, through them, the events of history." But, however illogical and however dull, it is obviously important that innumerable working-men have recognised in the account Marx gave of capitalist processes the experience they have themselves encountered. Any discussion of the Marxian system, therefore, must strive not only to state its theses in coherent form, but also to explain why they have aroused so much passion on their behalf. For even if they are wrong, the investigation of accepted error is always a clue to the wants of men.

II

The Marxian economic system is built upon two definite foundations. On the one hand, it is an amplification of that labour theory of value which, from its first faint beginnings in Locke, had become, in the hands of Adam Smith and Ricardo, the base of the classical economics, and, on the other, it is an argument that surplus values really due to labour-power are stolen from the latter by the

[1] *The End of Laissez-Faire*, p. 34.

capitalist. We shall discuss in this chapter the Marxian theory of value and seek to account for the form it assumed.

For Marx, the world of capitalism is a great heap of commodities. These must be wanted because they are useful, and they have therefore a kind of value we may call use-value. All business enterprise is built upon use-values. I produce what will be useful to other people because, otherwise, in a world based upon the division of labour, I cannot sell what I produce. Now what I produce comes to the consumer only after a complex series of exchange-operations. My commodity has not only a use-value for the person who is to consume it; it has also an exchange-value for the persons through whose hands it passes before it reaches the consumer. The consumer is only concerned with use-value; the producer, the wholesaler, the retailer, are concerned with exchange-value, with, that is, the amount of other commodities my commodity will exchange for. In the modern world exchange-value is price, and price is stated in terms of money. What determines the exchange-value, or price, of a commodity?

Marx begins by pointing out that use-values differ qualitatively, exchange-values quantitatively, from each other. I buy wine to drink, or books to read, or pens to write with. But when I buy any of these, the value I seek to know is the value-in-exchange. I consider wine as something for which other products, expressed in terms of price, must be given. I abstract all qualities from the commodity I purchase except that which is common both to it and to all other commodities. When this is done, I discover that the basis of exchange-value is "a mere congelation of homogeneous human labour, of labour-power expended without regard to the character of its expenditure." Value, then, is the amount of labour-time embodied in an article. It is the amount of labour which, in the average conditions of production, would have to be expended in order to reproduce a given commodity. Marx does not, it must be noted, say that value merely depends upon effort measured by time. He measures it in terms of what he calls "socially necessary" labour, the average time, that is, that the technical system of production requires. Should invention decrease that average, Marx does not deny that value would fall.

Labour, therefore, may be analysed from two angles. It has a use-value, which, in its concrete form, is the work of the miner, the clerk, the writer, or the stonemason, and it has an exchange-value, in which it is abstract, undifferentiated, homogeneous. Productive effort is the creation of exchange values by the expenditure of labour-power. The difference between different kinds of effort, skilled and unskilled, effort by brain and effort by hand, is quantitative; it is effort more valuable, perhaps, but attained by the expenditure of the same commodity, labour-power. Simple and unskilled labour, so to say, represents one "dose" of labour-power, skilled labour, two or three or ten "doses." Thus we can measure the amount of "labour-power" in each man's effort, and so determine scientifically how he ought to be paid. This is done by taking the commodity in which his effort is embodied to the market, and finding there its exchange-value. "It is only as they are exchanged," wrote Marx, "that the products of labour acquire as values a single and uniform social status which distinguishes them from the varied forms in which they exist as objects of utility." It follows, therefore, that value is fixed by the market. It is a co-operative act, in the determination of which buyer and seller combine. Neither can place his individual judgment of value upon the commodity; that is a function of the market judgment of the "socially necessary" labour it embodies.

Two remarks may here be made. It should be noted that Marx's definitions are wide enough to cover all labour-power that has exchange-value, whether mental or manual in character. Marx the agitator may sometimes have used sentences which seem to make his analysis more narrow than this, and to confiine the production of value to the working-class; but Marx the economist makes no such limitation. All effort, whether of manager, financier, worker by hand or brain, which is "socially necessary" in the production of an article, goes to make up its exchange-value. Criticism, therefore, which is built upon his failure to differentiate between skilled and unskilled labour falls to the ground. Nor is it vitiated by saying that it hardly explains, without strain, exceptional cases, like a First Folio of Shakespeare, or a precious stone discovered by chance. Marx intends the thesis, with perfect justice, to cover the normal cases of capitalist production.

But a difficulty arises here. Value, says Marx, is determined by the amount of socially-necessary labour-time embodied in a commodity; this amount is fixed by the process of exchange. But when the process of exchange is at work the terms of the equation seem to contain other elements than Marx allowed for. It is clear that if we say (1) that the value of a commodity depends upon the amount of socially necessary labour-time it embodies, (2) that this amount is discovered in the process of exchange, and (3) that the exchange-rate is fixed by the value of the commodity, we are really saying that value depends upon value. That is not helpful. And this Marx seems to have realised by admitting that over-production may reduce price by taking to the market for exchange a supply greater than the demand. He phrases the fact differently, indeed, by saying that, if the market does not take all the cloth woven by a weaver, " too great a portion of the total labour of the community has been spent in the form of weaving." But the result, however described, is that the proportion between supply and demand is a factor of importance in determining value. This, of course, is to say that the value is not merely a function of labour. It does not mean that labour is not an essential element in price; but it does mean that other factors must be taken into account.

Upon the basis, however, of this view of labour as the sole source of value, Marx erected his theory of surplus-value, which is the heart of his economic system. For what Marx, as a communist, had necessarily to do, was to show that there was a necessary and irreconcilable antagonism between master and man. This the surplus theory of value enabled him to attempt. At a certain stage in the development of society, he argues, there appears a class of free labourers. They are not serfs or slaves as in the past. They do not own the instruments of production, but they have their labour-power to sell. The capitalist buys this labour-power and sets it to work on the inanimate instruments of production. The resultant commodities are sold by him at a price beyond the cost of those instruments and the cost of the labour-power. It is, moreover, a characteristic of those instruments that without the application of human effort they are unproductive. Value, therefore, is a function of the human effort applied to them. Labour-power, that is to say, produces values above the cost of tools, raw materials, and its own cost. Marx calls this difference surplus-value, and points out that the whole of it is taken by the capitalist. Labour is therefore deprived of the surplus-value which it has itself created.

Why? Because, says Marx, the "value of labour-power, like the value of any other commodity, is fixed by the labour-time necessary for its production. . . . The value of labour-power is the value of the means of subsistence necessary to maintain the labourer." If five shillings a day enables X. to do his duties, then five is the value of X.'s labour. If X. works five hours to produce five shillings' worth of commodities, whatever time he works beyond that period will produce value in surplus for his employer. In fact, the worker does work beyond the period, and, accordingly, a system which purchases his labour-power, purchases also surplus-value, or profit, beyond the value of that labour-power itself. Wages, therefore, do not vary with surplus-value, but with the value of the labour-power which is not related to the amount of surplus-value produced.

It is clearly to the interest of the capitalist, by extension of hours, or other means, to increase surplus-values; thereby he gets something for nothing. Profit is therefore obtained by depriving the worker of all that he produces beyond the cost of his labour-power. Capitalism is therefore robbing labour as the law of its being.

Into the refinements of this analysis we cannot here go; but it is important to elaborate a little its central thesis. The basic and inanimate foundations of production—what Marx called constant capital—buildings, raw materials, machinery, produce nothing; productivity comes from what he called variable capital, the amount of labour-power expended upon them. It is therefore evident that in the production of any given commodity all who do not contribute labour-power thereto do not produce values. All, therefore, who receive part of the product without this contribution are parasites robbing labour. Marx accordingly denies that profit results from the capitalist who lends money or the trader who conducts the process of exchange.

The test of such a view is obvious. If surplus-value, or profit, is the outcome of variable capital, it must follow that the higher the proportion of variable capital in a concern, the higher must be the surplus-value, and inversely. Is this true? It is, as Marx himself pointed out, the invariable law of business enterprise that the rate of profit tends to equality, or, in other words, equal "amounts of capital, whatever the proportions of 'constant' and 'variable' capital within the amount, tend to produce equal amounts of surplus value." The law of surplus-value, as Marx said, "clearly contradicts all experience based on appearance." How is this seeming disharmony to be reconciled?

In Marx's own lifetime the solution did not appear. He himself was able to publish only the first volume of his great work; the two later volumes were edited from his materials by his faithful colleague, Engels. The explanation of the discrepancy offered by Marx appeared in the third volume. It was attributed there to the influence of competition. No individual, it was suggested, makes a rate of profit which coincides with the rate of surplus-value in his particular business; but the total mass of surplus-value is the measure of the average rate of profit. "The various capitalists," wrote Marx, "so far as profits are concerned, are so many stockholders in a stock company in which the shares of profits are uniformly divided for every hundred shares of capital, so that profits differ in the case of the individual capitalists only according to the amount of capital invested by each of them in the social enterprise, according to his investment in social production as a whole, according to his shares." Profits are thus a function of total surplus-values in the whole productive process. Marx compares the phenomenon to the position of a moneylender. " It is here," he says, " precisely as with the average rate of interest of a moneylender who lends out various parts of his capital at different rates of interest. The level of his average rate depends wholly on how much of his capital he has lent at each of the different rates of interest." While, therefore, profits as a whole equal surplus-values as a whole, the individual price of production does not vary with the ratio of variable to constant capital in a given business. But the tendency is for the law to become constantly more true as capitalism develops. For this development synchronises with a continuous increase in constant, and decrease in variable, capital as the mechanisation of industries becomes intensified. This makes the average rate of surplus-value more equal, and explains the approximation of profit to an equality.

It is clear that the explanation is hardly satisfactory. The Marx who, in 1865, was explaining that " the market-price of commodities will correspond . . . with their values as determined by the quantities of labour required for their production," and argued that profits come " from the sale of commodities at their values, that is, in proportion to the quantity of labour embodied in them," is propounding a very different theory from the Marx who is made by Engels to say that price is "a price of production equal to its cost price plus a percentage of profit apportioned according to the average rate of profit." Profits are then not only, as Marx himself admits, a function of surplus-value, but depend also upon competition. But this is fatal to the earlier view that things exchange in proportion to the amount of labour they embody. If capitalists "do not secure the surplus-value, and therefore the profit, created in their own sphere . . . but only as much surplus-value and profit as falls to the share of every aliquot part of the total social capital out of the total social surplus-value," then the competitive process compels them to accept less than their actual profits and prices are, at least in part, a function of competition. And this means that all surplus-value is not realised by anyone in the chain between ultimate producer and ultimate consumer until the latter is reached. We do not, in fact, know what the surplus-value is until we know the value in terms of price finally obtained for a given commodity. But this is again to argue that the value of an article depends upon what it fetches in the market, in other words, upon its value.

The explanation of the Marxian theory of value may be deferred while we examine the consequences Marx himself deduced from it. The business of the capitalist is profit or surplus-value. That is the motive by which he is dominated. To pursue it, he alters the character of the productive process. In its primitive stages, he finds the workers scattered, largely independent, imbued with the spirit of craftsmanship. He organises them into the factory system to extract surplus-value from their labour-power. Co-operation of labour produces higher productivity. Science is harnessed to the machine to intensify it. Long hours of labour result in a large surplus-value. But meanwhile there arises protest from the workers against their conditions. Their exploitation by the capitalist destroys health and leisure. Humanitarianism revolts against the transformation of women and children particularly into beasts of toil. The capitalist finds himself compelled to reduce the hours of labour, which produce what Marx calls "absolute" surplus-value; he therefore concentrates upon a more intense productive system by increased use of machinery and other labour-saving devices to secure, in the Marxian phrase, "relative" surplus-value. This means a decline, in the long run, of the labour-power required; more constant and less variable capital are used, with the creation of a surplus army of labour, and a lower rate of profit. This surplus army becomes that permanent reservoir of unemployed which characterises the industrial system.

Another effect follows. The greater use of constant capital means that the small capitalist lacks the means to compete with his more powerful neighbour. The concentration on "relative" surplus-value means, therefore, either the disappearance of the small trader, or the development of larger undertakings by means of combination. The means of production become, accordingly, increasingly concentrated in a few hands. The number of those who share in the distribution of surplus-value being continually smaller, the class of dependent wage-earners is constantly increased. And since this increase, with the reserve of labour it creates, is at best only partially employed, its function is to prevent excessive demands from the proletariat by creating a supply of labour in excess of the needs of the system.

Marx has set out in a vivid passage the consequences of this system. "All methods for raising the social productiveness of labour," he writes, "are effected at the cost of the individual labourer; all means for the development of production transform themselves into means of dominating and exploiting the producer. They mutilate him into a fragment of a man; they degrade him to the level of an appendage to a machine. Every remnant of charm in his work is destroyed, and transmuted into a loathsome toil; he is separated from the intellectual possibilities of the labour-process in the same degree that science, as an independent agency, becomes a part of it. They distort the conditions under which he works, and subject him, as he labours, to a despotism made the more hateful by its meanness. They transform his life-time into working-time, and his wife and child are dragged beneath the wheels of the Juggernaut of Capital. But all methods for the production of surplus-value are, at the same time, methods of accumulation; and every extension of accumulation becomes again a means for the development of those methods. It follows, therefore, that, as capital accumulates, the lot of the labourer, whether his wage be high or low, must grow proportionately worse. Accumulation of wealth at one pole is, therefore, at the same time accumulation of misery, agonised toil, slavery, ignorance, brutality, mental degradation, at the opposite pole, that is, the class which produces its own product in the form of capital."

The communist, it must be noted, does not deny that capitalism in its early stages represents a distinct and necessary advance upon the previous economic system. He is concerned, as Marx is here concerned, to point out that it contains within itself the seeds of its inevitable decay. For it is built upon inherent contradictions, and these must inevitably destroy it. Built upon the profit-making motive, its restless search for surplus-values makes it more and more dependent upon constant capital. This means a lower return, and to meet the problem thus created, capital continually concentrates. The middle-man and the small producer are crushed out; the growth of the reserve-army of the workers gives rise to over-population and a decline in demand through the decreased purchasing-power of the masses resultant upon the excessive supply of labour-power. Commodities, that is to say, are produced in ever-growing amounts, while the possibility of their purchase is ever declining. The outcome is over-production and under-consumption, with the ever-recurrent crises which are an habitual feature of modern civilisation. Capital is then wasted, production is restricted by monopoly and combination, the productive capacity of society ceases to be used for the common advantage.

Nor is this all. When Marx wrote his indictment, the potentialities of capitalism were only partly apparent. To-day, we see in imperialism and war its necessary outcome. Lenin, in his *Imperialism*, has completed the outline of its history. The increasing dependence upon constant capital means a struggle for access to raw materials carried out on a world-wide scale. Asia, Africa, the Pacific become the scene of struggles between competing capitalist groups backed by the power of their respective states. The necessity of vast expenditure in this effort leads first to the "personal union" of industrial and banking capital which gives a small financial oligarchy the control of the resources of the State. Monopolist capital grows by leaps and bounds. Everywhere it means the domination of trusts, the high cost of living, the "usurer State" in which the export of capital is the source of prosperity for a few at the expense of millions. It is a war of steel and gold, the consequence of which is the destruction of capitalism itself as incompatible with social good.

For upon the scale of its present organisation it depends upon the existence of an army of disciplined workers, habituated to receive unquestioningly its commands. But the workers, so far from obedience, combine to resist. Their wills and interests stand in antagonism to those of their masters. The narrow barrier which separate one group of workers from another is broken down as they realise that they have a common enemy in the class which owns the means of production. They begin to move towards the transformation of capitalism into communism. They realise that their labour-power cannot earn its just reward unless the means of production are owned in common. There comes, in Marx's classic words, "the revolt of the working-class, a class always increasing in numbers, and disciplined, united, organised, by the very mechanism of the process of capitalist production itself. The monopoly of capital becomes a fetter on the mode of production which has arisen and flourished with and under it. Centralisation of the means of production and socialisation of labour at last reach a point where they become incompatible with their capitalist integument. This integument is burst asunder. The knell of capitalist private property sounds. The expropriators are expropriated."

III

It is not difficult to understand the large measure of approval which the broad outlines of Marxian economics have received. Its message to the worker was an obvious one. The world was divided for him into those who lived by wages and those who did not. Those who lived by wages were, broadly speaking, poor, those who did not live by wages were, broadly speaking, rich. Assume, as Marx assumed, that the surplus theory of value is true, and the riches of those who do not live by labour are due to the poverty of those who do. The worker was able to see that he was poor. He saw, also, that he produced, collectively, more than he was paid, and that his surplus production was divided among a relatively small class of rich, and often idle, men. A theory such as Marx's naturally appeals to him as a simple explanation of his distressed condition. He clings to it, less by virtue of any logical explanation of its theoretic adequacy, than because it summarised vividly the most poignant experience he knew. The Marxian law of wages, moreover, will, from its very nature, win new adherents at every period of commercial depression. At any moment when there is a decline in the effective demand for commodities, or when the power of trade-union resistance is at a low ebb, the impact of capitalism upon the wage-earner will closely resemble what Marx insisted is its normal relation; for few business men have imagination enough to realise that there are other ways to the rehabilitation of markets than the reduction of price by means of lower wages. Inevitably, therefore, the worker will move from the acceptance of surplus-value to the philosophy which Marx constructed as its natural environment.

"Marx's theory of value and surplus value," writes a friendly German critic,[1] "has rather the significance of a political and social slogan than of an economic truth." But its errors must not blind us, as his opponents have often been blinded, to the large measure of truth contained in the deductions he drew from the theory. His insistence on the

[1] Max Beer, *The Life and Teaching of Karl Marx*, p. 129.

concentration of power in a few hands in the capitalist State has only partially been overthrown by his critics. It may be true that the growth of joint-stock enterprise distributes over a wider range the number of those interested in the receipt of profits; but it does not seriously touch the central problems of industrial control. There may be many minor industries, of which photography and the repair of motor-cars are examples, in which the tendency is to the increase of small firms rather than the development of large ones. But parallel with this evolution there has clearly gone an increasing tendency to monopolistic combination in all industries which require a large outlay upon fixed capital. Agriculture, indeed, despite the development of large-scale farming in Western America, and the encouragement of agrarian co-operation, remains persistently individualist in temper. Yet, on the balance of inquiry, it is impossible to deny the emergence of an increasingly corporate spirit in industry. And its reaction upon the workers is undoubtedly in the direction Marx foresaw. They develop a growing sense of unity, a growing desire to encroach upon spheres of control once deemed sacred to the capitalist. And if the expropriators are not, outside of Russia, expropriated, there comes a demand, in all industries of first-rate national importance, for socialisation. Capitalism seems at once to prepare monopolies and, in their operation, to be unable to retain the loyalty of the workers. The result is constant industrial conflict, and this affects the community towards a socialistic outlook as the one method of peace. No one can pretend to-day that the workers as a whole have any sympathy with the pretensions of capitalism. Especially do they feel that it is both ignorant and stupid to argue that the interests of workers and employers are identical. Such a view appears to them what John Stuart Mill termed "a goody morality."

For they have no patience with the people who, as Mill said, "think it right to be always repeating that the interest of labourers and employers is one and the same. It is not to be wondered at that this sort of thing should be irritating to those to whom it is intended as a warning. How is it possible that the buyer and the seller of a commodity should have exactly the same interest as to its price? It is to the interest of both that there should be commodities to sell, and it is, in a certain general way, the interest both of labourers and employers that business should prosper, and that the returns to Labour and Capital should be large. But to say that they have the same interest as to the division is to say that it is the same thing to a person's interest whether a sum of money belongs to him or to somebody else." On such a view, of course, once the facts of distribution are incompatible with social justice, the theory of class-war, upon which Marx laid so great an insistence, has a large measure of truth inherent in it. For the absence of justice in the division of the product may be held to imply a struggle for justice to which the parties are the sellers and buyers of labour-power. The conclusions, that is to say, which Marx built upon his theory of surplus-value are in large part true, even though the theory of labour-value is itself erroneous.

What, roughly, were those conclusions? They were, first of all, that the divorce of the masses from the ownership of the instruments of production must result, however large be the total aggregate of productivity, in poverty for those masses. That poverty will be intensified by insecurity and the fact that there are riches and idleness among those who share in the ownership of capital. To live by the sale of labour-power was, in Marx's view, simply slavery in a special form. There is not only inequality in the distribution of the product. There is, secondly, inequality in personal freedom. The poverty of the workers means that they and their children lack adequate access to knowledge, to justice, and to the sources of political power. Their intellectual environment is largely dictated to them by men who have different wants and different interests. Capitalism, thirdly, cannot maintain the initial successes which may be ascribed to it. It results, for reasons we have seen, in combination and in crisis. It damages the instruments of production by its wasteful use of natural resources. It is careless, as the necessity for regulation bears witness, of the human beings upon whose labour-power it depends. It adulterates the commodities it produces, thereby cheating the public and lowering the morale of those engaged in their production. The personality of those whom it employs is injured by the authoritarian control it exercises over them; as a system of government, that is to say, it is incompatible with the elementary principles of democratic government. As a consequence it provokes to revolt those over whose destiny it presides; internecine war is the law of its being, and this, in its turn, is fatal to the prosperity for which it was initially responsible. Finally, it leads to war by its need for the domination of foreign markets, the control of raw materials, and the protective tariffs for which it seeks in defence of its position at home.

It would be possible to extend this indictment to formidable length; [1] and even when the largest mitigations have been made, the broad outline of Marx's conclusions would be

[1] See Mr. and Mrs. Webb's *Decay of Capitalist Civilisation* for a brilliant statement of the position here summarised.

in sober fact unanswerable. Why is it, then, that economists, in general, have united to reject his views? The answer seems to be that the inadequacy of his theory of value has led them to infer that the conclusions he deduced from it are similarly inadequate; just as his supporters, recognising their own experience in his description of the capitalist process, have equally inferred that his ultimate explanation must be sound. But the errors of a great man are seldom without suggestiveness; and an examination of why Marx was led to his views will serve to explain something of the power they have exercised.

What Marx, it may be argued, was seeking was the criterion of a just exchange in a society where man obtains for the commodities he produces the ideal values he ought to obtain. He is building up a thesis which seeks to answer the case for capitalism as the latter was set forth by the classical economists. The latter, as is well known, derived their views from the theory of value first outlined by Locke. In the *Second Treatise on Government* Locke defended private property by arguing that a man is entitled to that with which he has mingled his labour. He envisaged a society in which the individual is entitled to what he has because by his own effort he has wrung it from the caprice of Nature; that, for Locke, is the real justification of possession. But, obviously, Locke's natural society is not the society we know; and a system which accounts for ideal values, while it may be used to test the existing values of a given society, is not necessarily an explanation of them. What Marx does is to take over from Locke the idea of a society where each man, subduing Nature to his own wants, earns what he is worth, and applies its criteria to the society about him. But the characteristic of the latter is the introduction of economic relationships which do not subsist in the former; and the theory of value which describes the first cannot, of course, describe the second.

But Marx is here, of course, simply repeating what the classical economists had already sought to do. As with Adam Smith, Ricardo, and, above all, MacCulloch, they had used the labour theory of value to describe the complicated society they knew on the assumption that competition was perfect and that monopoly was non-existent. They assumed, in other words, that perfect equality existed as between the buyers and sellers of labour; what each class received was what each class earned. It was then simple to argue that the reward of the capitalist was just. And the step from this highly abstract society to the one about them was a simple one, the more so because the removal of legislative restrictions seemed likely to create the perfect society of *laissez-faire* theory. The labour theory of value, so regarded, became above all a justification of profit.

Now Marx's business, as he conceived it, was to accept the basis from which the classical school started, and to turn its results against them. He seeks to show that, on their conditions, the labour theory of value leads to socialism, because an historical analysis of capitalism makes it evident that while it is an endeavour to render to each man his own, in fact it renders increasingly to a few much more than their own, and to the many much less. It is the parent of inequality, and that at a time when, largely as a result of the French Revolution, "the notion of human equality has acquired already the fixity of a popular prejudice." Capitalism and equality being in conflict, and the latter being destined to an inevitable triumph, it follows that capitalism is merely a stage in the evolution towards socialism where, by reason of the common ownership of the means of production, each man will again receive his own.

It is clear, then, that at the root of Marx's view there lies an ethical test of value. Commodities, for him, have not merely use and exchange values; they have also an inherent value which is what they would obtain in exchange where society was properly organised, that is, where the equality of primitive society obtained. And the measure of the difference between this inherent value and the actual exchange value of contemporary society is for him the measure of the degree to which labour is deprived of its rights. For this inherent value, assuming equality, enables production and social need to be directly proportionate to each other. Such a society would obviously be just; whereas the fact of inequality means a society inherently unjust because the relationships between supply and demand are perverted by the failure to adjust them to social need.

In other words, Marx, is constructing a theory of value in terms of natural rights, and he sees that the equation between them cannot be effected unless value is regarded as a social product. Yet the individualist society he knew, even more the thesis he was seeking to overthrow, was essentially a denial of that view, and an endeavour to trace back the creation of value to persons regarded as independent. Marx saw that the independence was untrue, and he attempted, accordingly, to utilise an individualistic theory of value for the discovery of conclusions that have a social implication. But the only way in which he could utilise that individualism was by regarding it as an ethical criterion constantly perverted by the capitalistic process. Hence his theory of value constantly passes from ideal criterion to realistic description without the transition being marked certainly in his pages, and possibly in his mind. He put his finger on the essential weakness of the theory he attacked, but at the expense of importing into his description of capitalism a judgment alien from the abstract assumptions from which he starts.

It is here, of course, that there lies the attractiveness of his view for those who have experience of the results he describes. In a society of equals where the producer of commodities also exchanges them, it is clear that the return to him is proportionate to his effort if what he produces is socially necessary. But in a society of unequals, where the division of labour produces a differentiation between production and exchange, this is no longer the case. The profits of exchange cannot now be identified with the rewards of the producer. Yet the theory of profit in the classical economists is based upon the assumption that this is the case. Nor is this all. The wage-earner, in contemporary society, has no measurable commodities to exchange. He sells only a labour-power which, broadly speaking, has to unite itself with the labour-power of others to produce; and there is then no longer the means of differentiating the contribution of each wage-earner to the total product. Yet the classical theory of wages, ignoring this, argues that what the wage-earner receives is what he produces, exactly as though he were the joint producer and exchanger of primitive and equal society.

The wage-earner, of course, sees that he is in fact producing more than he receives, and that this surplus-value is profit. He therefore agrees with Marx that he is robbed.

It is, of course, easy to show that in the simple form that Marx gave to his view, the doctrine is indefensible. He sometimes speaks, for instance, as though exchange is incapable of creating value, though he himself knew quite well that this is not the case. But if Marx treats the profit-maker with contempt, he might reasonably argue that the classical economists treated the wage-earner no differently. And having made good his case that value is a product of social relations, that, in other words, it is impossible to trace back the creation of any definite part of value to a given producer, he is entitled to insist upon his criticism of capitalist society that its system of rewards has no relation to justice. That is so because it is built upon inequality; and the really central plea of Marx, and the effective source of attraction in his economic system, is his demand that economic relationships be built upon the basis of equality.

Put briefly, Marx's economic philosophy is a demonstration that in a society where the few own the instruments of production, and the many have nothing to sell but their labour-power, the theoretic results of freedom of contract which the classical economists predicted cannot possibly occur. For those theoretic results depend on an equality of bargaining power which, by a magistral analysis, he showed to be absent from the society about him. And not only absent, but, from causes that were undeniably operative, it was bound to be absent in increasing degree. Capitalism made men unfree by the governmental process it involved. For it denied the ideal of equality without which democratic government is impossible. As the child of the French Revolution Marx had no doubt that the ideal of equality was desirable, and his thesis was a challenge to the orthodox economist to show why the assumptions they made in politics ought not to be applied to the process of production. Therein he expressed, with a wealth of learning, the half-conscious sense of the wage-earner in his daily life. For the fascination of Marx in this aspect is exactly his attack upon the inequality of the existing regime; and it is only by the remedy of that inequality that his hold over the minds of men is likely to grow less.

IV

This explanation, it should be added, does not make the Marxian theory of value defensible as an economic analysis. The fact rather is that, in the form Marx gave to his theory, the problem he confronted is, *ex hypothesi*, insoluble. For immediately we assume that value is a social product, is, that is to say, the result not of individual, but of co-operative effort, we cannot trace the individual contribution of any man to the sum-total of production. For the co-operation makes productivity something more than the sum of the individual efforts that have gone to its making. The division of labour, therefore, involves activities of a nature which, by destroying the assumptions of the labour theory of value, make that theory itself otiose. The results of Marxism, in fact, and, it should be insisted, its driving power, really come from the fact that it demolishes the foundations of an individualistic society.

It does not, indeed, replace them except by arguing that justice in economic arrangements can only come from the common ownership of the means of production and a theory of reward conceived in terms of capacity and need. Marx's scientific instinct taught him to avoid the danger of Utopia-making; and his firm grasp of the idea of evolution made him realise that the changes he foresaw in large outline would bring with them novelties in detail he could not foresee. He was, if our own experience is any guide, wrong in his belief that the breakdown of capitalism would give place to a comparatively simple society; we have come increasingly to realise that our very scale of life, whatever the economic system, involves complexity. And once it is admitted that no society can endeavour to assess the individual contribution to its wealth as the basis of reward, it is clear that theories of reward will shift to a very different foundation from that postulated by individualism. Whether, as some imagine, the impossibility of tracing the individual contribution makes equality of reward the only equitable hypothesis we are not called upon here to inquire. What it is alone important to realise is that in adopting Marx's theories as its own, communism acquired an economic philosophy which, though in part erroneous, has the strength that comes from building its appeal upon some of the profoundest impulses of men.

CHAPTER IV

THE COMMUNIST THEORY OF THE STATE

I

MODERN social organisation is built upon the division of the world into a number of independent and sovereign States. These present always the phenomenon of a large number of people owing obedience to a small number of themselves organised as a Government. To the latter is confided the ultimate control of the national resources. It makes and administers the laws. The naval and military forces, the police-system, the foreign policy of the State, are set by the terms of its will. The forms of Government may, indeed, vary. In England, the State is a constitutional monarchy of which the Government is chosen indirectly by universal suffrage; in America it is a republic with power divided centrally between a legislature and an executive independently elected by the people as a whole, with local authority controlled upon a similar basis; in Spain and Italy the prevailing system is a dictatorship which, in the case of the latter, masks itself under semi-constitutional forms. Whatever be the nature of political institutions, their central fact is always the legal duty of the many to obey the few, with the right of the few to exercise the power at their disposal to compel obedience.

What is the *raison d'être* of the State? In the classical theory, it exists, broadly speaking, to secure the good of society as a whole. It provides a plane where men may meet as citizens without regard to differences of race or class or creed. All other associations are partial in character; trade unions, churches, employers' federations, absorb the allegiance only of a few, and exhaust that allegiance but partially. The State differs from all of these in that membership of it is compulsory, and that its Government strives, or ought to strive, to hold a just balance between the different elements in society. It strives by its policy to effect such an adjustment of the relationship between citizens as will enable each of them to realise, if he so desires, the fullest implications of human personality.

Obviously, such a view of the philosophy of the State is a doctrine of ideal ends rather than of assured purposes. The State, like all other human institutions, has a history; and it is not to-day what it was yesterday, or will be to-morrow. To say, for example, that Tudor England sought to provide the conditions under which the average Englishman could realise the fullest implications of his personality would be to talk plain nonsense; and it is not less obvious that in our own day the vast majority lack, through no fault of their own, any such opportunity. The answer of those who accept the classical view is to argue that while the State has not yet achieved its end, it is in continuous process of doing so. Conditions are better to-day than they were a hundred years ago; they will be better again to-morrow. The political process, on close scrutiny, reveals a continuously closer adjustment of institutions to human desires; and, especially where democratic government prevails, the State is in the hands of the people to mould as they will.

It should be added that this view does not represent the doctrine of thinkers in general, even among those who reject communism. Roughly, it is built upon a belief in the desirability of liberty and equality. Philosophers like Linguet, de Maistre, and Bonald have denied that these are either possible or desirable. They have argued that, on the contrary, the sacrifice of the well-being of the many to the interests of the few is a necessary feature of social organisation; and, in the case of Maistre and Bonald, they offer the consolations of religion to the many as a reward for their subordination. Certainly it must be said that there is this much of truth in their view that at no period in history has the well-being of the masses been consciously the chief motive in public policy; and if the many are necessarily to be subordinate to the few, it is not improbable that organised religion alone has the authority over men's minds adequate to make them accept their lot.

There is an interesting resemblance between the theory of the State held by reactionaries like de Maistre, and that of Marx and his disciples. Each holds that the subordination, and even suffering of the masses, is a necessary consequence of social organisation, and each holds out a prospect of ultimate benefit to them as a recompense. But whereas with de Maistre and his school, that recompense is found in the next world, the Marxians offer hope in this by picturing the State as an organ of repression and urging that liberation can be won by its overthrow. The analysis by which the communists have reached this position has at least the merit of simplicity. Capitalist society, they argue, is built upon the deliberate exploitation of labour by the capitalist. The latter possesses all, and commands by reason of his possessions; the worker has nothing and obeys because he has nothing. Why is such an order of society tolerated? Mainly, it is said, for two reasons: first, because the capitalist is organised and powerful, and, secondly, because he is able to control the ability of the workers

The chief means by which it maintains its organisation is the State. "In all countries," urges Bukharin, "the State is merely a union of the master class. . . . Everywhere we find that the ministers, high officials, Members of Parliament, are either capitalists, landowners, factory owners, and financial magnates, or else the faithful and well-paid servants of these, lawyers, bank managers, professors, army officers, bishops, who serve the capitalists not from fear but from conviction." The union so composed has, says the communist, broadly two aims. It seeks, in the first place, to secure the capitalist class in the possession of the means of production. For this purpose exists the immense apparatus of law and police, and, in the last instance, the armed forces of the State. In capitalist States the laws of treason and sedition, for example, are, from a communist standpoint, so defined as to make rebellion and urgent criticism of the possessing classes difficult to the point of impossibility. The Criminal Law has been, in general, more severe upon offences against property than upon offences against the person because capitalism is more tender to the interests of property than to those of human life. The second aim is to compete with other States, which, similarly, are organisations of the master-class for a larger share of the results of the productive system. "The capitalist State," Bukharin concludes, " is a union of the master-class formed to safeguard exploitation. The interests of capital and nothing but the interests of capital—here we have the guiding star towards which are directed all the activities of this robber band."

In technical terms, then, the communist regards the State from two points of view. As an economic organisation he sees it as a society of capitalists for the extraction of surplus-value from the workers; as a political organisation it is for him a society to protect the process of extraction from rebellion by the workers who suffer from that process. Throughout the political process it will be found upon examination that the organs of the State are directed towards no other end. Even the administration of justice, he insists, is deliberately perverted to serve the ends of capitalism. The German State sends Liebknecht to prison because he threatens its security; but it has no difficulty in acquitting the murderer of Liebknecht. So, also, the communist holds, with what may be termed the means of spiritual subjugation which the State possesses. The schools, he thinks, serve as deliberate training-grounds of obedience and order. The children of the workers are taught there the wickedness of rebellion, the splendour of Kingship, the duty of worshipping as heroes the soldiers of the nation. Men who sought the truth, like John Ball, are execrated, while those who, like Wellington, were the paid servants of reaction, are held up as models to emulate. The Churches, to him, enforce a similar lesson. By insisting that all power comes from God, they seek to make rebellion identical with blasphemy. They teach men to accept their lot without repining instead of calling upon them to throw off their chains. And the Press is always at hand to distort the facts, to insist upon the inevitability and justice of the present régime, to fasten still tighter the chains upon its victims. "The Capitalist State stands on guard and takes good care that there shall be no uprising of the wage-slaves."

The rôle of the State is thus, in the communist view, an essentially simple one. It is "the product," says Lenin, "and the manifestation of the irreconcilability of class-antagonisms. Where, when and to what extent, the State arises, depends directly on when, where and to what extent the class-antagonisms of a given society cannot be objectively reconciled. And, conversely, the existence of the State proves that the class-antagonisms *are* irreconcilable." This view is essential to communist doctrine. Its exponents will have no compromise such as has been sought by reformist socialists with the purpose of showing that the State can seek to reconcile such antagonism. Order, for them, is merely a halt between a collision which has passed and a collision which is to come; to seek the means of reconciliation is merely to deprive the working-class of the means whereby it can free itself from oppression. For the State being simply the force at the disposal of capitalists, and capitalists being the instruments of oppression, to reconcile the workers to the State is to reconcile them to oppression in perpetuity. When, for example, the Independent Labour Party in England inquired, in 1920, from the Third International whether communism could only be introduced by armed force, the answer they received left no room for doubt. "The workers should prepare," wrote the Executive Committee of the Communist International, "not for an easy parliamentary victory, but for victory by a heavy civil war; should the workers have succeeded in gaining power without this civil war, that would only signify that the necessity of civil war would confront the working-class so soon as it set out to realise its will to defend itself from capitalist exploitation and speculation, so soon as it began to liberate the masses in the colonies now oppressed by British Imperialism."

On the communist hypotheses, therefore, the ideals which the modern State announces are inherently incapable of realisation. The fact of economic exploitation as the basis of the existing social order makes the substance of things like justice, liberty, equality, void of meaning; they cannot be secured by an organisation of which the purpose is the domination of the majority by the minority, of the oppressed by the oppressors. The root of the modern State is force used to prevent exactly the achievement of the end announced by the State; and, consequently, the only way to its accomplishment is the seizure of that force by those who are now excluded from the benefits it secures. It will be noticed that the unstated metaphysic of communism is a very simple one. The goods at which the State aims are not denied to be goods, it is simply insisted that the organisation which seeks them is a flat contradiction of its aims. And, on the analogy of the Hegelian dialectic, it is only by the negation of the State that men can enter into their kingdom.

Nothing, perhaps, so well illustrates the communist attitude to the State as its analysis of modern democracy. The protagonists of the classic theory point out that in the democratic State each individual citizen has the franchise; he is equal with all other citizens before the law; no barrier stands in the way of his entrance into whatever career he may choose. Since Governments are made and unmade by the electorate, since, that is, they rest upon opinion, it is only necessary to convert the majority of the electorate to communism for the authority of the State to be used to apply it. Were that to occur, a communist Government would come into office, and if its will were to meet with resistance it would utilise all the legal authority at its disposal to destroy opposition and impose its ideas. Communism is therefore possible of application within the limits of constitutionalism.

The communist does not deny that, at a certain stage in the historic process, the democratic State has a real, though limited value. The criteria it establishes make possible the awakening of the masses to a consciousness of their position. Democracy as the condemnation "of absolutism, aristocratic privileges, and the property qualification" defines the fighting ground between capitalist and proletariat. It provides the opportunity for organising the power of the workers into trade unions and political parties. But this utilisation of the mechanisms of democracy does not imply its acceptance as "an unshakeable principle."

For the more closely it is examined, the more false that principle appears. The idea of natural rights inherent in the individual, and of equal application to all, is merely fiction. "You are deprived," cries Trotsky to the worker, "of the possibility of realising those rights. Conditional and shadowy legal equality has been transformed into the convicts' chain with which each of you is fastened to the chariot of capitalism." For no amount of ideal right will make the ignorant tiller of the soil the equal of Rothschild. "The landlord, the labourer, the capitalist, the proletarian, the minister, the boot-black, all are equal as 'citizens,' and 'legislators.' The mystic equality of Christianity has taken one step down from the heavens in the shape of the 'natural,' 'legal' equality of democracy. But it has not yet reached earth, where lie the economic foundations of society."

Consider, the communist insists, not the ideal claims, but the actual facts. In the ideal democracy all men are free and equal, to teach, to speak, to write as they please, to vote as they will, to apply communist principles in practice. "There is not," writes Lenin, "a single State, however democratic, which does not contain loopholes or limiting clauses in its constitution, which guarantee the bourgeoisie the legal possibility of dispatching troops against the workers, of proclaiming martial law, and so forth, in case of the disturbance of public order. That is, in case of the 'disturbance' by the servile class of its servile condition." The majority, in fact, has the right to enforce respect for its rights upon the saving condition that it does not exercise it. The American negro is the equal of the Southern white; amendments to the American Constitution guarantee his freedom and his franchise. Yet he dare not exercise it. The majority of the British electorate desired Home Rule in 1914; they were met with rebellion in Ulster when they sought to give effect to their desire. The American citizen is guaranteed freedom of speech by the Constitution; and the power of the mails and the police power of States and cities is used to suppress it whenever it proves inconvenient to the established order. The masses, everywhere, desire peace; what they receive is a secret diplomacy which makes wars in the interests of capitalist bandits and deludes them with fine-sounding talk of national honour and national interests. No man is barred from access to wealth, or learning, or position; but the fact remains that those who reach them are pitiably few in number.

Or, consider, the communist urges, the mechanisms of justice. All men are equal before the Courts; but they cannot enforce their equality save by the possession of wealth they do not possess. The humble tenant who seeks redress against his landlord, the servant girl who is dismissed without wages or character by her mistress, the workman injured in the course of employment and refused compensation by an employer who argues negligence on his part, all these are but instances of an inequality before the law which gives the lie to the democratic thesis of equality. The hierarchy of courts, moreover, may well swallow up in the costs of appeal even the pitiful redress the worker has been able to secure. The very fact that special legal institutions have been created which seek to alter the balance the present order maintains is itself proof that the democratic claim is inadequate.[1]

We must remember, further, the growing degeneration of the classical democratic institutions. "In proportion as the mass of citizens who possess political rights increases," writes Lafargue, "and the number of elected rulers increases, the actual power is concentrated and becomes the monopoly of a smaller and smaller group of individuals." "Such," comments Trotsky, "is the secret of the majority." Everywhere, it is evident, legislatures have declined in either authority or prestige. Either, like the English Parliament, they become the creature of the executive, or like the legislatures of France and America, their conflict with the executive prevents them from making an effective policy. The boss in America, the caucus in England, these simply organise masses of voters to carry out the choice upon which they have determined. An American president is not made by the people; they merely select

[1] Cf. for a well-balanced view of the actual position of the law and the poor R. Heber Smith, *Justice and the Poor* (New York, 1920), and E. A. Parry, *The Law and the Poor*. They measure very fairly the degree of truth in the communist indictment summarised above.

one of two men whom a handful of organisers in either party has decided upon as a satisfactory figurehead. The voter cannot be influential in electorates of the modern size; the deputy is little better off. Power in the modern democratic state passes to a small number of efficient wire-pullers who understand how to control the machine. And every legislature is so overwhelmed by business that it has no time to discuss adequately any important question. What, in short, is interesting in representative Government is not its anatomy, but its pathology.

Nor does the communist accept the theory of majority rule that is implied in the democratic hypothesis. What happens, he points out, in the modern State is the conflict of minorities with the mass of the people remaining inert or acquiescent. The real will of the latter is never known. What it might be, if the facts were in its possession is obscured by the miasma of lies and brutality and propaganda which surrounds its life. When, for instance, Kautsky criticised the Bolsheviks for their refusal to call the Constituent Assembly and accept its decision, he forgot that since the latter was formed before the real significance of the November Revolution was known, that decision could not have represented popular desire. The communist, in short, represents what the proletariat would will if all the facts were in its possession. In refusing to take account of the apparent will that alone can express itself through democratic forms, he is forcing the real will of the worker into action. In Rousseau's terms, he forces the worker to be free.

This view of minority-action is of great importance in the political theory of Bolshevism. Left to the theory of democracy, the people cannot free itself, and yet it wills its freedom. The communist party represents that will. It seeks the end—the social ownership of the means of production—and it cannot, therefore, reject the means. Since constitutional methods cannot secure the end, it follows, on the communist view, that unconstitutional methods must be used.

II

The communist attitude to violence is set in the perspective both of history and of theory. Historically, they take their stand upon the assumption that the State is the embodiment of force. Whatever the temporary equilibrium that may have been attained, its life depends upon the use of armed force to protect its purposes. That is why, for example, it punishes so severely all attempts on the part of the working-class to persuade the army and navy to its cause. Take away from the State its instruments of repression, and it could not last for a moment. It lives only by the compulsions at its command.

Historically, moreover, force has always been the essence of revolution. In the Reformation, for example, religious precepts were victorious to the degree that military power was behind them; and the more bitter the wars waged on their behalf, the more thoroughgoing was the terror used to give them point. The English revolutions of the seventeenth century were both won only by the use of the sword. The classical revolution of 1789, says Trotsky, brought with it "a corresponding classical terrorism"; and it is patent that without the iron dictatorship of the Jacobins the republic would have been destroyed. When the Southern States were defeated at the election of 1860, they did not hesitate to use force to secure the perpetuation of slavery; and in the war that ensued both they and their opponents used every sort of method, constitutional or unconstitutional, to achieve their ends. The failure of the Commune, in 1871, was mainly due to its unwillingness to utilise the force its position required. "The enemy," so Trotsky writes, "must be made harmless, and, in wartime, this means that he must be destroyed." History shows that the capitalist has risen to power, has consolidated his authority, and maintains his pre-eminence in this way. Revolution gives him power; civil war consolidates his authority : and repression or dictatorship enables him to retain it.

From facts such as these, the theory emerges clearly; and its truth is reinforced by the history of the Russian Revolution. If you desire to conquer, you must have the will to conquer. That will does not mean passing resolutions at conferences, where you convince your friends by your eloquence. It means imposing your will upon an enemy who will use every means at his disposal to defend his entrenched position. Revolution is not exactly war, but its central problem is the same as in war. Its makers must assume the offensive. They must forcibly break the will of the enemy and impose upon him acceptance of the ends for which they are fighting. They cannot assume that the inherent justice of their cause, or the numbers on their side, will persuade a ruthless enemy to surrender without making an effort to win. "The question as to who is to rule the country," writes Trotsky, ". . . will be decided on either side, not by references to the paragraphs of the Constitution, but by the employment of all forms of violence. . . . (There is) in history no other way of breaking the class-will of the enemy except by the systematic and energetic use of violence."

The communist, in fact, is compelled to be realistic. Willing the end, he cannot wipe his hands of the means. The problems before him are not, unless he condemns, like a Quaker, all forms of violence, questions of principle, but of expediency. He kills and imprisons not for the sake of killing and imprisonment, but because, first, he would himself be killed or imprisoned otherwise, and secondly because thereby he forces millions to accept the consequences of his will. There is no purpose in seizing power if one is to be hurled from it; and it is the clear outcome of history that only determined use of force can avert this. "A revolutionary class," says Trotsky, "which has conquered power with arms in its hands, is bound to, and will, suppress, rifle in hand, all attempts to tear power out of its hands. Where it has against it a hostile army, it will oppose to it its own army. Where it is confronted with armed conspiracy, attempt at murder, or rising, it will hurl at the heads of its enemies an unsparing penalty." If it is said that the terrorism of the communist does not differ from the terrorism of the Tsar, the answer is that the principle for which communists use terrorism is different. "The gendarmerie of Tsarism throttled the workers who were fighting for socialism. Our extraordinary commissions shoot landlords, capitalists and generals who are striving to restore the capitalist order. Do you grasp this distinction?" asks Trotsky; "for us communists it is quite sufficient."

No one who has studied at all carefully the history of the Russian Revolution will doubt that the communist means by violence all that the term can imply. By violence he seizes power, and by violence he defends himself from attack. Since he has to impose his will upon the conquered, he takes what he conceives to be the shortest means to that end. He justifies the method by the greatness of the purpose for which he is contending, and by the argument that experience shows no other road to success. Things like the White Terror, the murder of Liebknecht and Rosa Luxembourg, the Allied Blockade, the invasions and civil wars, all make it clear that he has not misinterpreted the nature of the problem that confronts him. He denies accusations, like that of Kautsky, that to use terrorism is to "betray the principle of the sacredness of human life." That is betrayed if one executes a murderer; it is betrayed by war; above all, it is betrayed so long as labour, and therefore life, under the capitalist system, is a commodity to be bought and sold. "As for us," writes Trotsky, "we were never concerned with the Kantian priestly and vegetarian-Quaker prattle about the 'sacredness of human life.' We were revolutionaries in opposition, and we have remained revolutionaries in power. To make the individual sacred we must destroy the social order which crucifies him, and this problem can only be solved by blood and iron."

The argument that the end justifies the means, however, does not represent the whole of the communist position. "If," it might be said, "the communists use violence and are justified by their purpose in so doing, any other party which has, similarly, a great purpose, would be similarly justified." The communist does not accept this view. From his standpoint, the revolutionary violence of communism differs from all other violence by reason of the historic position it exploits. A White Terror in Hungary, for example, is merely the effort of capitalism to postpone the coming of communism. It cannot effect more than a postponement. Since the workers are, historically, the rising, and the capitalists the falling, class in society, revolutionary violence is force used to further the natural evolution of society; violence used against communism is violence used in the service of reaction. "The Red Terror," writes Trotsky somewhat naïvely, "is a weapon utilised against a class, doomed to destruction, which does not wish to perish." This animal, in other words, is naughty; when it is attacked, it defends itself, without realising that its skeleton is needed for a museum of specimens.

It will be noticed how profoundly the communist theory of violence is bound up with its theory of historic evolution. It is not a justification of violence as such. On the contrary, violence is regarded as a *sæva necessitas*, inevitable simply because the bourgeois State does not surrender without giving battle. It is useless, say the communists, to fight unless you are going to win; and it is useless to win unless you propose to use your victory to serve the interests for which you fought. Your terrorism is justified because you, a rising class, are fighting the bourgeoisie, a falling class, with the weapons they have made an inherent instrument of the conflict. Their violence, on the contrary, is futile, except as retardation, simply because they have not the future on their side. Communism, that is to say, is made superior to capitalism by the logic of history. And, at least in the long run, the assurance of its triumph makes the use of violence worth while because, in the classless state, it is no longer necessary; whereas bourgeois violence, by being only an instrument of postponement, simply increases the amount of force that is necessary to attain the inevitable end.

III

By violence, then, the communist captures the State; and by the replacement of the dictatorship of the capitalist by the dictatorship of the proletariat he consolidates the position so acquired. What is the theory of communism as to the period of transition intervening between the fall of capitalism and the establishment of a Communist Society?

No question has been more warmly discussed in recent years. Largely speaking, it has assumed the form of a contest over the meaning of Marxism between Kautsky, the leading German socialist, and the Russian communists. Into the details of the debate it would be fruitless here to go. Largely, indeed, it may be said to have arisen because violence had become abhorrent to Kautsky, as to most humane people, through the horrors of the War, and its deliberate use by the Russians made him recoil in horror from the literal meaning of the Marxian record. He sought, therefore, an allegorical interpretation; words, phrases, connotations were subject to an exegesis of which the purpose was to prove that by the dictatorship of the proletariat neither Marx nor Engels meant the abandonment of democratic ideals nor the use of terrorism upon the scale the Russians were willing to attempt. The latter, and especially Lenin and Trotsky, had little difficulty in disposing of Kautsky's argument. No one can read the discussions by Marx and Engels of the period of transition without seeing that though they had no prevision, and could have had no prevision, either of the scale of the struggle, or the instruments it would demand, what they had in mind was a methodology such as the Russians adopted. In any case, the Russian technique has become the classical formula of communism; and debate upon the meaning of Marx's terminology has to-day little more than an historical interest.

So interpreted, the communist view would seem to be upon the following lines. The State arose as an instrument of class oppression; when classes disappear, the State will disappear also, since its *raison d'être* will have gone. "When organising production anew on the basis of a free and equal association of the producers," wrote Engel, "Society will banish the whole State-machine to a place which will then be the most proper one for it—the museum of antiquities side by side with the spinning-wheel and the bronze axe." But the banishment, of course, is not accomplished overnight. The communist has no use for the anarchist demand that the State be destroyed because it is an instrument of coercion, and all coercion bad. The State does not disappear in a flash; it "withers away." But that process is a long one, and no one can set out the limits of its duration.

It is, however, possible to describe the general features which will distinguish the process of change. The proletariat will, as we have seen, take possession of the State by means of revolution. Its first act, when it possesses the authority of the State, is to socialise the means of production. "But by this very act," wrote Engels, "it ends itself as a proletariat, destroying, at the same time, all class-difference and class-antagonisms, and with this, also, the State. . . . The first act of the State in which it really acts as the representative of the whole of society, namely, the control of the means of production on behalf of society, is also its last independent act as a State. The interference of the authority of the State with social relations will then become superfluous in one field after another, and will finally cease of itself. The authority of the Government over persons will be replaced by the administration of things, and the direction of the processes of production. The State will not be 'abolished'; it will wither away."

This paragraph contains the heart of communist reflection upon the period of transition. In the Russian exegesis, it summarises the experience of Marx and Engels after reflecting upon the meaning of the revolutions and especially the Commune of Paris, they had known. It distinguishes, as a doctrine, between two States. There is the *capitalist* State which exists at the time of the revolution itself; this is simply destroyed. There is, also, the *proletarian* State which exists to see that the destruction of its capitalist predecessor is final; this, little by little, disappears, as its work of destruction is consolidated. What, then, is the distinction between the "destruction" of the one and the "withering away" of the other? The central institutions of the capitalist State, it is explained, are the army and the bureaucracy; these are the main instruments by which the Capitalist State had achieved its purpose. They have to be broken in pieces because, from the standpoint of the proletarian revolution, the fact that they were devised for a different end leaves them without meaning. "The Communist learns from the experience of 1871," said Marx and Engels in their preface to the last joint edition of the *Communist Manifesto*, "that the working-class cannot simply seize the available ready machinery of the State and set it going for its own ends." "The next attempt of the French Revolution," wrote Marx to Kugelmann in 1871, "(will be) not merely to hand over, from one set of hands to another, the bureaucratic and military machine—as has formerly occurred—but to *shatter* it."

What, then, replaces the capitalist State as so destroyed? What, in other words, are the features of the proletarian State? It cannot be said that Marx himself gave us any clear answer to the question. In the *Communist Manifesto*, as Lenin admits, we hear only that the proletariat will be organised as the ruling power. In the *Civil War in France* the experience of the Commune enabled Marx to provide some further details. The standing army is to be replaced by the nation in arms, which means, on communist theory, that part of the nation which accepts, in communism, the real will of society. The police are to lose their political functions and to be made responsible to, and replaceable by, the new State. So also with the officials in different parts of the administration. "From the members of the Council of the Commune down to the humblest worker, everybody in the public services was paid at the same rates as ordinary working-men." Privileges disappeared; the power of the priests was broken; the judiciary lost "its sham independence," and became subject to election and recall. "Democracy," comments Lenin, "carried out with the fullest imaginable completeness and consistency, is transformed from capitalist democracy into proletarian democracy; from the State (that is, a special force for the suppression of a particular class) to something which is no longer really a form of the State."

So far, what is achieved is, first of all, the elevation of the majority to a power which enables it to suppress, instead of being suppressed. Secondly, the reduction of officials to the level of the general population, especially in the matter of wages, enables the ordinary man to secure a full share in discharging the functions of the State. The abolition, thirdly, of the standing army, and its replacement by the army of the proletariat, ensures the defence of the revolution by men committed to its doctrines. The principles, finally, of election and recall of officials make these directly responsible to the authority which creates them. If this seems to savour of the ideals of primitive democracy, the answer of the communist is that this is necessary in the period of transition from capitalism to communism. For otherwise, neither can every individual in the population share in government, nor can we destroy the glamour of the old government itself. This primitive democracy, moreover, differs from its early prototypes in that on the basis of scientific discovery and organisation, the governmental process can be easily simplified once the means of production are socialised. In 1919, indeed, Lenin even believed that they might be brought within the reach of every literate person.

It goes, of course, without saying that parliamentary institutions must disappear also. Marx in 1871 had already pointed out that the Commune was to have been " not a parliamentary, but a working corporation, legislative and executive at one and the same time "; and Lenin drew therefrom the inference that the Soviet system was a higher form of institution and far more suitable for revolutionary effort. The Soviet was, in essence, a council of soldiers, workmen, and poorer peasants, which combined, in the communist view, all the advantages of the territorial principle, with the additional benefit of making the natural cell of representation the unit of production to which the proletarian voter belonged. Local soviets combined in a series to produce regional and provincial soviets; these, in their turn, were linked together to form the central soviet assembly which was the main legislative body of the proletarian State. It was rendered flexible by the device of the recall; it was kept revolutionary, first by limiting the electorate to the actual producers, and, secondly, by dominating the elections themselves by the Communist Party. Formal democracy, that is to say, was compelled to give way to what the communist calls "the revolutionary dynamic of living forces"; by which seems to be meant that the exclusion of all non-working-class elements from the electorate, and the control of the remainder by the communists produced an instrument of decision which the latter could make entirely responsive to their will. And this was justified because the communists represented the real will of the electorate, the things they would desire to see done had they been able to achieve communist ideas.

In the transitional period, indeed, the essence of the communist position is that the rule of the working-classes, or, in the classic phrase, the dictatorship of the proletariat means, and can only mean, the dictatorship of the Communist Party. "The condition of an efficient struggle for the dictatorship of the proletariat," Bukharin told the Fifth Congress of the Third International, "is the existence of a Communist Party, firmly welded together, accustomed to fight, disciplined and centralised. . . . These parties must direct the working-class struggle in every sphere and take advantage of every possibility that offers to bring the workers under their influence." For in the vast medley of associations, economic, cultural, political, there is no other way of maintaining the necessary unity of direction. The Communist Party will, it claims, contain the élite of the working-class. It is, communists say, by all odds the best school for training leaders who can dominate the variety of proletarian organisations. It knows, as no other body can know, how at once to liquidate the class-war and to transform non-partisan associations into bodies which are useful for this purpose. The Communist Party, in short, is in the view of its adherents, proletarian organisation at its best. It is the vital instrument, without which power cannot possibly be maintained. It enforces discipline and organisation upon the masses. It breaks that terrible conservatism of habit in which tradition otherwise enfolds a society of millions. "Without a party of iron," wrote Lenin, "tempered to the art of conflict, and enjoying the confidence of all the honest elements in the working-class, knowing how to observe and to influence the spirit of the masses, such a conflict as ours cannot be conducted."

The party, moreover, must have a single mind and will. Its power therefore depends upon the absence of faction within itself. "As the civil war becomes the more fierce," it is laid down, "the Communist Party can only accomplish its task by being highly centralised. Its discipline must be of iron, and almost military in character; and it must be ruled by a central committee with wide powers." This does not, indeed, imply that there is to be no discussion or difference of opinion in the party; no one who knows the history of the Russian communists can doubt that their policy is arrived at after debate as eager and vivid as that of any party in the normal bourgeois State. What its discipline means is that there must be no dissent from decisions once they have been taken. To be beaten in debate means to accept the results of defeat and to co-operate as loyally with your conquerors as if it was your own view which had prevailed. "In the Second International," says Stalin, "the parties thereto can admit sectionalism; Communists cannot permit themselves this luxury since their object is power." That is why, at the tenth meeting of the All-Russian Congress of Soviets, Lenin carried a resolution " for the immediate dissolution of all groups based on one or another platform under penalty of immediate exclusion from the Party," and it is a logical inference that all opportunists who incline to doubt, or to alliance with non-communist elements in society, must be similarly excluded. " Hesitation when the call to battle comes," wrote Lenin, " may lose everything . . . therefore the loss of those who hesitate, so far from weakening, actually strengthens the party, the movement, and the revolution."

IV

The communist, then, marches to power by an assault upon the bourgeois State. Once captured, it is transformed by a dictatorship which is, in fact, the iron rule of the Communist Party. It then becomes the transitional proletarian State which is to " wither away " as the advent of communism renders it otiose. What are the methods of transformation? Here, at least, the observer has a task of great difficulty. There is a distinction of primary importance between the programme of communist transition and the actual changes accomplished; and there is ground for genuine disagreement as to whether the actual achievement may be regarded as the preparation for the ultimate ideal. For some communists, indeed, the new economic policy of Lenin, whereby a large measure of private trading was admitted, was definitely a break with the legitimate practice; for Lenin himself, it was a necessity in the light of the actual situation, but a necessity which was itself purely temporary in character. And, in any case, the original theory remains as the foundation to be adapted to particular situations. Any communist revolution, it may be said, will have to insist at least upon certain things. It will have to confiscate all great industrial enterprises like electricity, railways and engineering. It will have to nationalise the great landed estates, while leaving to the peasantry sufficient land to neutralise their possible hostility to the new régime. The banks must be taken over, and with them the gold reserve; small depositors may be granted interest. All wholesale commerce must be nationalised; and foreign trade must become a monopoly. The State debts should be repudiated. The working-class must monopolise all important journals and printing-presses. As a general rule, small, or medium-sized businesses need not be nationalised, partly because the new State will rarely, at least at first, be able to run them, and partly because it is futile to think of establishing communism at one blow.

Measures must be taken to associate intellectual technicians with the new régime and to neutralise the peasant-class; the poorer peasants should be carefully organised, while care must be taken to repress any possible opposition from the richer. So, also, with the poorer bourgeoisie of the towns; and its goodwill can probably be bought by leaving to it what it has, by granting it economic freedom, and protecting it from the need to hire capital at usurious rates of interest.

What is the position of the individual worker in the transitional State? We must note, first, the obligation to labour; "He that will not work shall not eat," is the elementary rule of communist society. And to end the anarchy of capitalism, the economic life of that society must be organised as a whole. The worker cannot choose what he will do; he must labour as the State decides. His protection will be found in the safeguards provided by the different labour organisations to which he will belong. These will discuss on his behalf questions like wages and hours of labour, the sanitary condition of factories and so forth. They must, of course, function under the ægis of the Communist Party; for, otherwise, they cannot effectively fulfil their rôle in the transition period. The worker will have technical education at his disposal; and efficient work, as in the Taylor system, will win a special reward. But of industrial self-government in the sense, for example, that guild socialists use the word, there can be no question. " No board of persons who do not know the given business," writes Trotsky, " can replace one man who does know it. . . . A board in itself does not give knowledge to the ignorant. It can only hide the ignorance of the ignorant." Direct management by the individual is necessary to evoke responsibility, initiative and rivalry in the capacity for service. The workers' protection is found in criticism of results, in publicity of accounts and productivity, in the power, through trade union or political party, to make his wants felt at the source of authority. He is, in short, organised for the benefit of society instead of being exploited for the benefit of the capitalist. " Socialist economy," writes Trotsky, " . . . is founded on the thinking worker endowed with initiative." It is the business of organisation, when it discovers this initiative, to give it room for action in the background of the rules laid down by those who control the State. The individual, in other words, is subject to the technical situation; the technical situation is not the creature of the individual. Thereby, as the process of education achieves its end, a communist economy is constructed side by side with the State, ultimately to replace it. But until that stage is reached, the " road to Socialism," as Trotsky says, " lies through a period of the highest possible intensification of the principle of the State."

To the outsider, it may be observed, this looks not unlike the rigorous suppression of the individual personality. In a sense, this is true; but it is important to realise the communist answer to the charge. It argues, first, that his position is at least superior to what it is in a capitalist economy. There, at least, he can neither in fact choose what he will be, nor can he be assured of employment. In the transitional proletarian State, he may not choose, but he is assured of being maintained so long as he is willing to work. And the fact that he cannot choose is offset by the knowledge that the work he does counts in the degree of its quality towards the coming of the ideal; while the ability he shows may open to him a larger avenue of power. His standards, moreover, are set for him not by the will of the employer but by the will of the proletariat as the latter is interpreted by the communist dictatorship with a view to the needs of the situation. Should he, finally, belong himself to the Communist Party, he can have his share in moulding the views of those in whom power is vested.

So much may be said upon the industrial side. But it must not be forgotten that communism, even in the period of transition, claims to bring what may be termed spiritual advantages to the proletariat. Exactly as capitalist control of the means of production is suppressed, so, also, is capitalist monopoly of education. In every aspect of life, it is necessary, if the proletariat is genuinely to direct the new society, that it should be fully trained to the largest tasks. This means not only the instruction of specialists, but also the general raising of the level of working-class culture. In the arts, the sciences, in politics, it must have the first right to the training at the disposal of authority. Such education must, of course, from its earliest stages be definitely communist in spirit. In bourgeois society, education was intended to prevent the workers from realising that they were slaves; in the proletarian State it must be used to teach them that they can be masters. " In the realm of the mind, in the psychological sphere," says Bukharin, " the Communist school must effect the same revolutionary overthrow of bourgeois society, must effect the same expropriation that the Soviet Power has effected in the economic sphere by the nationalisation of the means of production. The minds of men must be made ready for the new social relationship. If the masses find it difficult to construct a Communist society, this is because in many departments of mental life, they still have both feet firmly planted upon the soil of bourgeois society." Education, in short, is to become an instrument of propaganda for the communist regeneration of society.

Closely allied to this educational effort must go a campaign against the bourgeois superstition of religion. It is necessary here, the communist admits, to go carefully, since above all in the working-class, the power of religion has been immense. But Marx's famous phrase, "religion is the opium of the people," sets the temper of communist purpose. Religion and communism are incompatible since social development, as the laws established by historic materialism have shown, is not affected by supernatural forces. There is, moreover, an incompatibility between the commands of most religions and the tactics of communism. Christianity, for example, with its emphasis upon the duty of submission to the powers that be, and its precepts of self-abnegation stands definitely in the way of an offensive against the bourgeoisie.

The conflict with religion has two sides. It is, relatively speaking, easy in the transition period to separate the Church from connection of any kind with the State, and, by inference, to abolish its relation to, and influence in, the schools. By making religion a purely private matter, and offering it no assistance from public authority, its prestige is visibly shaken at the outset. The nature of education in the schools, moreover, works to render the minds of the children "immune to all those religious fairy-tales which many grown-ups continue to regard as truth." But this is only one aspect of the problem. More difficult is it to fight the deeply-rooted prejudices which cling to life long after their exposition as folly. Here, in the communist view, a long period of slow erosion lies ahead. Religion, in this sense, will ultimately die partly by deliberate propaganda against it, partly also by the general diffusion of education, which is, in the long run, fatal to its authority. But, above all, the communist relies upon victory as a result of the change from capitalist to communist society. The former favoured religious prejudice simply because the nature of its processes was so largely hidden from the worker. He did not know what was happening or why it occurred. It was easy to tell him, and easy for him to believe, that all was due to the will of God; and thus to persuade him to accept beliefs and support an organisation which purported to possess a monopoly in God. But with the coming of communism the processes of social organisation will no longer be mysterious. The worker will see not only the little piece of work he performs, but the whole system of relationships of which it is a part. "Throughout the entire mechanism of social production," writes Bukharin, "there will be no longer anything mysterious, incomprehensible, or unexpected . . . the mere fact of the organisation and strengthening of the communist system will deal religion an irrecoverable blow. . . . The transition from the society which makes an end of capitalism to the society which is completely freed from all traces of class-division and class-struggle, will bring about the natural death of all religion and all superstition."

The communist, it should be added, does not conceal from himself that the victory of the proletarian State depends largely upon its ability to display a superior economic productivity to that of its capitalist predecessor. Lenin and Trotsky, above all, have been insistent that the first task of the proletarian government is to overcome the natural laziness of man. "The problem before the social organisation," says Trotsky, "is just to bring 'laziness' within a definite framework, to discipline it, and to pull mankind together with the help of methods and measures invented by mankind itself." To this end a variety of means, compulsion, propaganda, payment by results, demands for volunteers, surrender of the normal standard conditions are to be used. Trotsky himself even attempted the actual militarisation of labour, though, it appears, with inadequate success. They bring to this task the same superb self-confidence which distinguishes their effort elsewhere. They assume, in the first place, that the mere fact of a transition to communism will, of itself, evoke new effort from the worker. They deny that compulsory labour is wasteful, once the bourgeois ideology has disappeared. The new sense of equality, the constructive character which the effort of each man acquires in the new conditions, makes obsolete all earlier discussion about the higher premium to be put upon "free" labour. The explanation to the worker of why he must work harder under the new régime than under capitalism is sufficient to secure from him a full response. For he will realise that the system of wages will disappear as increasing productivity enables the State to guarantee to all the workers the necessaries of life. He will labour the more earnestly to achieve that end. Compulsory labour is the road to communism. The new State will perish unless that is understood; and the need to understand it will evoke the will to a successful conclusion.

V

Let us assume, at this point, that the problems of the proletarian State have been solved. The resistance of the capitalist enemy has been completely liquidated; the production of the new régime is satisfactory; the moment, in fact, has arrived when the "withering-away" of the State has so far advanced, that complete communism is obviously possible. What will be the dominant features of the new society? To what criteria are we to refer for an understanding of its nature?

We are here, of course, in the realm of prophecy; and, with wisdom, neither Marx nor his disciples attempted to emulate the detailed and unconvincing Utopias fashioned by their predecessors. They were unanimous that the time required for the disappearance of the State would be long, and that it will depend upon the development of productivity by the new institutions. But, quite rightly, they insist that neither time nor form for the completion of the new order can be given. All that it is possible to say is that the character of the new society will be set by the formula: From each according to his powers; to each according to his needs. The new society will come, says Lenin, "when people have become accustomed to observe the fundamental principles of social life, and their labour is so productive that they will voluntarily work *according to their abilities*. . . . There will then be no need for any exact calculation by Society of the quantity of products to be distributed to each of its members, each will take freely 'according to his needs.'"

We are not, further, to assume either "the *present* productive powers of labour," nor "the present unthinking man in the street, capable of spoiling, without reflection, the stores of social wealth, and of demanding the impossible." The day of compulsion will have gone. Men will give freely of their best, and receive, equally freely, the best in return.

We do not know the outlines of this new society in any greater detail. We can assume that the proletarian dictatorship has been an immense education for the masses. They will have grown accustomed, in the first phase of the revolution, to all men working, and to equal pay. They will have seen the reduction of governmental operations to simple functions which anyone can understand. " The whole of society," writes Lenin, " will have become one office and one factory, with equal work and equal pay." Class-distinction and economic exploitation will have gone. Public functions will have been converted from the acts of a State into merely administrative functions.

When that stage arrives, we may expect the formal end of the State. It is perhaps best, for the sake of accuracy, to explain the situation in Lenin's own words. " When all," he writes, " or be it even only the greater part of society, have learned how to govern the State, have taken this business into their own hands, have established a control over the insignificant minority of capitalists, over the gentry with capitalist leanings, and workers thoroughly demoralised by capitalism—from this moment the need for any government begins to vanish. . . . For when all have learned to manage, and really do manage, socialised production, when all really do keep control and account of the idlers, gentlefolk, swindlers, and such-like 'guardians of capitalist traditions,' the escape from such general registration and control will inevitably become so increasingly difficult, so much the exception, and will probably be accompanied by such swift and severe punishment . . . that very soon the *necessity* of observing the simple, fundamental rules of any kind of social life will become a habit. The door will then be open wide for the transition from the first phase of Communist society, to its second higher phase, and along with it, to the complete withering away of the State."

One cannot, of course, criticise the impalpable, and it will be sufficient, at the moment, to bring out the unstated assumptions of this view. The use of fear is to bring submission; with submission willl emerge new habits that destroy the oppression and acquisitiveness characteristic of capitalist society. Freedom from exploitation will make possible a greater willingness to work well. Education will achieve an understanding of social needs sufficient to make unnecessary the institutions of compulsion characteristic of the old régime. The new society will ultimately be richer than the old because of the new powers it can realise; and it will not need to read the terms of its contract with its members as though this were Shylock's bond. The reader of Hippolyte Dufresne's vision of the new society in M. Anatole France's *Sur la Pierre Blanche* has, perhaps, an adequate insight into its conditions.

Two other remarks may be made. It is important to remember that the communist regards this new society as the outcome of a long evolution; he offers it as an ideal to be achieved by a later generation than our own. It comes when grim conflict is over, and the lesson of suffering has been learned. When, secondly, he explains that government will be unnecessary, he is not pinning his faith to a Godwinian anarchy. He believes in organisation as much as any of his critics. But he believes in an organisation which has grown out of an acceptance of natural law from below, not from a capitalist law imposed from above. The State which withers away does not leave men in a relationship of primitive discreteness. It is the capitalist State as the organ of exploitation that disappears, and, with it, the habits engendered by the capitalist State. The regulations which take their place are built upon consent instead of force; and since, to the communist, force and the State are synonymous, he feels justified in speaking of its obsolescence.

VI

The first comment one is tempted to make upon communism as a theory of the State is that, like most philosophies, it is strong in what it affirms, and weak in what it denies. Obviously enough, its criticism of the assumptions of the classical theory of the State is, in part at least, well founded; the margin between the ideal and the real is a large one. It is, moreover, true that no ruling class in history has so far surrendered its privileges, or utilised its authority for the common good, without a struggle. Men cling to power even after the grounds which make its tenure intelligible have passed away; and there is a real basis for the assumption that the holders of power in a capitalist State are no exception to the rule. And, not less certainly, there is substance in the communist criticism of formal democracy; the mere conference of universal suffrage and the creation of representative institutions will not, of themselves, secure the kind of State which adequately safeguards the claims of men upon the common good.

But it is one thing, and it is not a new thing, to affirm the imperfections of the present social order. It is different, and much more dubious, to argue that the only way to alter those imperfections is by violent upheaval, and that, even ultimately, from violent upheaval is born an idyllic society. Revolutions rarely succeed in achieving their original aim; they cannot tread a path that is indicated by an *a priori* system of conditions. Those who direct them may be compelled to give way before demands which destroy their original demands. The leaders who seize power for one end may choose to maintain power for quite different ends. Or they may be unable to meet the forces of counter-revolution, and the new condition may be worse than the first. The means, moreover, involved in the use of violence may so enter into the original end as completely to transform its nature. "The revolutionary leader," wrote Lord Morley, of Cromwell, "treads a path of fire." At least it is certain that he cannot know where he is going. The forces he is compelled to loose limit his direction and alter his possibilities at every turn. He is confronted, broadly speaking, by three problems. There is the problem of initial success—the actual seizure of power. There is the problem, secondly, of consolidating the positions that have been gained; after ten years the Russian government is still in this phase of revolutionary effort. There is the final problem of creating the new society in terms of the promised ideal. Each of these phases involves considerations which the communist is inclined, perhaps too easily, to brush aside.

The preparation for revolution is a qualitatively different problem in our own day from what it was in the days of the Paris barricades. It was possible for civilians, as in 1871, to hold up a military force hardly better or differently equipped from itself; that was the experience from which Marx drew his conclusions. It is possible for a civilian population in a mood of defeat to destroy a régime which the forces at the disposal of the government no longer uphold; and, as was demonstrated long ago by Cromwell, a military force which is dissatisfied with its civilian superiors can easily become their master. That was Lenin's circumstance in 1917, and he took advantage of his position with consummate insight. But for a party of men in the position of communists in the modern State the position is very different. Unless they are the majority, and, consequently, the government, the hostility of the army and navy is certain. Nor can they obtain, on any large scale, the necessary equipment for insurrection. They would have to obtain control of the national arsenals; and that would mean the dispersion of forces in any case small by hypothesis. They would have to possess, and know how to use, the weapons of chemical and aerial warfare; and their possession of them alone would argue, under modern conditions, a government devoid of authority. They would have to meet in the people at large at least a mood of acquiescence. They would have to guarantee a supply of food which, in any but a predominantly agricultural society, would be practically impossible if the state credit were seriously impaired—as that of Russia was impaired—

by the revolution. Even if we regard a general strike as a revolutionary weapon, the difficulties in the way of its success are overwhelming. It might succeed as a protest against war, by arousing emotions of determination that would be irresistible. But upon any other issue, it seems tolerably certain that, once again, the army and navy must be in the control of the strikers if success is to be assured. For a modern army can supply all services connected with transportation; it can secure the distribution of food, and the problem of fuel is no longer dependent upon the mining of coal. The communist theory of a secretly armed minority assuming power at a single stroke, is, in fact, unthinkable in the modern State if the army and navy are loyal to the government. It would have to imply either a government so weak that it had practically ceased to be a government at all, or, what is perhaps equivalent, a population actively sympathetic to the revolutionary minority. The resources of publicity in modern civilisation make impossible the preparations in private of the gigantic effort implied in the communist thesis.

But this is only the beginning of the problem. States, as the communist realises, are not independent of other States. England, for example, with her dependence upon foreign trade could not undergo a successful revolution unless her neighbours view its results with benevolence. America is unlikely to adopt such an attitude, and the rupture of Anglo-American trade would be fatal to an English revolution. If Russia then came to the assistance of England, we should merely see a world-war in which there would be disaster equally from victory or defeat. Certainly the outcome, on any showing, would so impair the resources of civilisation as to make the advent of communism a matter for the Greek Kalends.

Nor is this all. The sectionalism a revolution implies will be only partially determined by economic considerations. In a country like America, for example, there would be at least three other factors of vital importance. An American communist revolution would have to cope with problems of distance which would probably render it abortive at a very early stage. It would not, as in France, be a matter of the immense impact of the capital on the life of the nation; a communist rising in Washington, even a simultaneous rising in New York and Boston, would be a headline in the newspapers of the Pacific coast. To control the whole continent would involve controlling the most complicated and extensive railway system in the world; and to do that successfully implies a degree of sympathy with the revolution which would render its occurrence unnecessary. Yet even if that difficulty could be surmounted, a complex of national differences would have to be assuaged. German, French, English, Irish, Polish, these have their special characteristics which the American capitalist has been able to exploit to their common disadvantage; it is difficult to see how an appeal to the communist minority of each would result in the transcendence of these differences. Even then, the religious problem remains; and the hold of the Churches, particularly, upon the mind of the Latin peoples, would not be easy to loosen. And even if it be argued that the day of such prejudices as nationality and religion is passing—which may be doubted—and that the barriers built by economic difference are alone important, the communist conclusion is surely dubious. For in a period of universal suffrage, it ought then to be possible to capture the seat of power at the polls, and throw upon the capitalist the onus of revolt against a socialist democracy. For that would associate with the socialist government not only its active supporters, but that large section of people in every modern community who, desiring to be let alone, believe profoundly in constitutionalism; and while at the best it would retain the services of the army and navy, at the worst it would so divide them as to neutralise its greatest opponent.

There are other aspects of the problem which, it may be argued, the communist does not adequately consider. There is, in the first place, the general result upon society of the practice of violence, particularly in the light of the destructive nature of modern warfare; and, in the second, there is the special psychological result upon the agents of the opposing forces in a revolution. The communist does not meet this merely by insisting that the use of violence is inevitable and that it will be worth while. Such an attitude fails to weigh sufficiently the necessary substance of a political psychology and is the corollary of a determination which the facts hardly justify. For it is obvious that if revolution is justified to the communist merely because that is *his* logic of history, it will be justified also in any other people with a cause which they deduce from *their* logic of history; and no community can then hope either for security or order. Every argument, that is to say, which justifies a communist revolution justifies also a Fascist revolution, at least to those who are convinced Fascists. The war has shown clearly that the impulses of savagery which are checked by peace are, when loosed, utterly destructive of the foundations of a decent existence. If life became an anarchic jacquerie, civilisation could quite easily be reduced to the State where, as in Mr. Wells' imaginary but far from impossible picture, some aged survivor may tell of an organised Europe as a legend which his grandchildren cannot hope to understand.

Violence on the grand scale, in fact, so far from proving an avenue to communism, would be the one kind of existence in which the impulses demanded by a communist society would have no hope of emergence. For the condition of communism is the restraint of exactly those appetites which violence releases; and the communist has nowhere shown how this difficulty can be met except by affirming that dictatorship will destroy them. That is the argument from the power of repression; and it is sufficient answer to argue that the survival of communism in a world of capitalist repression is itself proof that repression is futile.

Even beyond this issue, a further point must be raised. The communist assumes the seizure of power, and a period of rigorous control until the people are prepared for communism. But he is ignorant of the time the dictatorship is to last, nor does he explain why those who control it may be expected to accede to its termination. It is a commonplace of history that power is poisonous to those who exercise it; there is no special reason to assume that the communist dictator will in this respect be different from other men. Indeed no group of men who exercise despotic authority can ever retain the habit of democratic responsibility. That is obvious, for example, in the case of men like Sir Henry Maine and Fitzjames Stephen, who, having learned in India the habits of autocracy, become impatient, on their return to England, of the slow process of persuasion which democracy implies. To sit continuously in the seat of office is inevitably to become separated from the minds and wants of those over whom you govern. For any governing class acquires an interest of its own, a desire for permanence of power, a wish to retain the dignity and importance of its functions; and it will make an effort to retain them. That, after all, is only to insist that the exercise of power as such breeds similar habits in its operators. The corollary of dictatorship appears to be that which follows from all other systems—that it is incapable of voluntary abdication. The only way to prevent this is to educate the people in government by associating them with the act of governing. But this is to postulate the undesirability of dictatorship.

Further difficulties remain. It is not easy to see why the transition period between capitalism and communism should create the atmosphere out of which the latter develops, if, as in Russia to-day, the small trader, the specialist paid at a special rate, the peasant owning and working his own land, a system of special interests is created which may counteract the education in communist ideas which goes on alongside with them. Nor must we omit the effect on the people in this period of the absence of liberty and equality. The communist may be right in denying their reality to-day; and he may, further, be justified in insisting that their absence explains the dumb acquiescence of the multitude in a system which denies them their rights. But in the transition period they must either acquiesce or be destroyed by the dictatorship; that alternative surely is only the exchange of one tyranny for another, neither of which will breed the habits of freedom. And if it be said that communist tyranny is conceived in the interest of all, the answer obviously is that the interest of all can only be known when all share in proclaiming it; and it is the purpose of the dictatorship exactly to prevent this by the suppression of views and movements it dislikes. It prefers its own view of what men ought to think and do to what, in fact, they do think and do. Historic experience suggests that this cannot produce an erect-minded people; and it suggests further that all attempts to force a people into a Procrustes' bed of preconceived ideas, however well-intentioned, is doomed to failure. The experiment, after all, is not new in history; it is the old attempt to insist that certain laws are too important ever to be legitimately revoked. Calvin in Geneva, the Jesuits in Paraguay, were the victims of the same illusion; and their effort was a warning rather than an example.

Nor can it be said that the communist indications of the ultimate goal are very enlightening. There is the problem, first, of seeing exactly how a system which comes as the harbinger of all those evils from which we are seeking release can prove the forerunner of their antithesis; unless, indeed, we insist, upon *a priori* grounds, upon assuming the objective reality, as a social process, of the Hegelian dialectic. Nor, secondly, is it easy to see why the destruction of capitalism should result in a classless society. It might, on the contrary, mean a society divided into a class of directing communists, and the rest; or, as Mr. Bertrand Russell has suggested, a class which insisted upon short hours of labour and a low productivity and one which desired longer hours and a high rate of reward. Marx and Lenin were doubtless right in arguing that a new system of production will emphasise new tendencies in human nature. But we cannot say without experience either that they will be better tendencies or that they will be precisely the tendencies a communist society requires. That affirmation is no more than a prophecy which may be justified in the event; we are even entitled to attempt experimental proof of its truth. But we are not entitled to assume that it has about it anything of the rigorous exactitude of scientific law.

The governing rule of the communist

society, we are told by Marx and Lenin, will be the formula, " From each according to his powers, to each according to his needs." For the purposes of rhetoric that is doubtless an admirable canon; but it is worth pointing out that it is incapable of precise meaning. For we cannot measure powers, especially in the realm of intellectual effort; and the only criterion of needs that is possible is one that assumes a rough identity between men and the insistence that the claim of this identity upon the social product is the first charge we must recognise. We require, in brief, an objective test of powers and needs; and this means the discovery of a social average which rejects the individual differences of which, by implication, the communist formula professes to take account.

It is, moreover, worth while to remark that most communist writers immensely over-estimate the simplicity of politics. Their picture of institutions which have been rendered so simple in their operation that the average man can understand them at once, fails to take account of the complexity of society and builds upon the belief that the average man is generally and continuously interested in the methods by which it moves along its way. It is obvious that the division of labour, whatever the distribution of the product, and the nature of the services to be maintained if the scale of life is to remain at its present level, do not permit simplicity. It is one thing to grasp the principle that the supply of electricity must be nationalised because it is too important to remain in private hands; granted a decent level of education, no one supposes that the ordinary citizen can mistake the character of the argument. But it is a very different assumption, and much more questionable, that the average man can, without prolonged investigation, decide which of a variety of systems of nationalisation is suitable to the service of electricity supply. And, whatever the type of society, those willing to attempt such examination are likely to be few. Man is not by nature a political animal. He gives his attention rather to the results than to the methods of institutions; and he gets interested in methods less for their own sake than because of dissatisfaction with their outcome. That the degree of his interest, and its continuity, may be largely increased by institutional improvement need not be denied. But it is a long step from that belief to a vision of a society which is widely devoted to the constant scrutiny of its political process.

It may be quite true, as the communist argues, that social justice is unattainable through the ordinary institutions of representative government. No one, certainly, who is careful of historic truth will argue that its victory is likely to be easy. But we are not entitled to act upon the assumption of its impossibility until we have made much further experiment than has so far been attempted. We can at least say of the alternative to the trial of parliamentarism that it involves a long epoch of bloody war in which success is problematical and defeat disastrous; and we can say of parliamentary government that it has notable successes to its credit. The rights it has established are shadowy and unsubstantial compared to any programme of adequacy. This is certainly the main strength of the communist indictment. Yet it is surely obvious that there is no justification for the resort to violence until the resources of reason have been exhausted. The resort to violence, even if it be successful, means trusting the officials who control the application of violence. It does not mean liberty; it does not mean equality; and it does not mean justice. It means the despotic application of power by men whose intentions, however admirable, are the creatures of circumstances. The chance that the transformation of values so necessary to the attainment of justice will take place as a result of blood and iron is a very tenuous one. The barbarian invasions of Rome did not produce a great epoch of enlightenment; they produced the dark ages. The Thirty Years' War impeded constructive effort in Germany until the threshold of the nineteenth century. The idealism of 1914 has perished before the greater strength of the destructive forces released in the struggle. That is why it is permissible to doubt whether the method of violence is ever the midwife of justice. That wrong can be wiped out with wrong is a gospel to which we are not entitled to resort until we despair utterly of civilisation; and when we have resorted to it, it is probable that there will be no civilisation of which to despair.

Nothing of this, it should be added, implies that the communist prediction of conflict is impossible of realisation. The evils which have led to its diagnosis are real, and their remedy alone is a specific against economic war. For a point is reached in the development of any social system where men will refuse to accept longer a burden they find too great to bear; and in that moment, if they cannot mitigate, they will at least destroy. The condition, in fact, upon which a State may hope to endure is its capacity for making freedom more widespread and more intense. It is not easy to achieve that end. Men prefer sacrifice by others to the surrender of their own desires. To choose equality, in Matthew Arnold's phrase, has been the exception in history; and societies have fallen because they have lacked the courage to flee from greed. It may be that a similar experience will be ours. If it is, the fault will lie neither at the door of the communist, nor of the ordinary man. The former has been a warning to the rulers of the modern State that consistent reformation is the only effective answer to the challenge of the extremist; and the latter is too patient and long-suffering to revolt unless there is real justice on his side. The communist theory of the State, that is to say, has so much of justice on its side that the proof of its wrongness lies, above all, in the demonstration that its ideals can be realised by alternative means. That requires effort rather than assertion; and the effort must be forthcoming soon, if it is to reach its appointed end.

CHAPTER V

THE STRATEGY OF COMMUNISM

I

SINCE the communist regards the present system of social relationship solely in terms of class-war, it is only logical that he should adapt the strategy of the movement to its making. It is, moreover, essential in considering both the theory which underlies, and the institutions which express, this strategy, to realise that it is with a world-battle that the communist is concerned. Because capitalism is a world-phenomenon, the revolution that is to secure its overthrow is necessarily a world-phenomenon also; for revolution is implied in the historic logic of capitalism.

The communist, indeed, does not say that revolution will come everywhere either at once or in the same way. Here it may arise because organised labour makes demands upon the propertied interests which the latter dare not grant; there it may be the response to an attempt at drastic and resented wage-reductions; in one State, again, it may come in resistance to an effort by the government at imperialistic war; or, as in Russia in 1917, in the aftermath of a similar conflict. All that can be said is that a declining capitalism will present a series of possible revolutionary situations and that, whatever the failures, the ultimate catastrophe will one day come.

It is obvious, in this background, that communists must prepare themselves for the conflict in these world-terms. The pivot of their movement has, accordingly, been the Third International, and the separate national movements are built around its centre. The Third International serves a variety of purposes. Partly, and perhaps pre-eminently, it is the ultimate deciding body in the world-communist movement; its broad conclusions embody the policy which all affiliated parties must accept. It provides, so to say, the outlines of the communist way of life in a capitalist world; it decides upon the means whereby that world may be destroyed. Partly, also, it is a propagandist body. Its business is to prepare the way, by publications, by the training and organisation of agents, along which the army of communism is to move to victory. Partly, also, by giving a centralised character to the efforts of communists in different States, it prevents the dissolution of the movement into a disconnected series of particular efforts; for it is obvious that such separation might destroy the effects of the unified support which, properly organised, the movement as a whole can bring to bear upon the activity of the parts. This centralism, moreover, is strengthened by the capacity of the International to give financial aid to its constituent branches. Finally, it has the task of preventing, within the ranks of any single communist section, that tendency to fractionalism and dissent, so fatal to the development of a united fighting front.

From its inception, and quite naturally, the residence of the Communist International has been at Moscow; the attitude to it of capitalist governments would have made its continuous activity impossible elsewhere. Its purpose is best defined by its statutes. It aims, it is there laid down, at "the organisation of common action between the workers of various countries who are striving towards . . . the overthrow of capitalism, the establishment of the dictatorship of the proletariat and of the International Soviet Republic, the complete abolition of classes, and the realisation of socialism as the first step to communist society." Its ultimate governing instrument is the World Congress. This body meets at least once a year, and, in addition, as often as either its executive, or a demand from one-half of its affiliated members may deem necessary. It does not appear that the World Congress has any fixed system of membership. Communist parties in capitalist States are, in general, in too difficult a position in relation to access to Russia to make a rigid structure desirable. The constitution of the International, therefore, merely lays it down that "each section shall have a number of votes which, by the decision of the Congress, represents its effective strength and the political importance of the country concerned." The Congress also elects the President of the International, the executive committee, and a special non-political body called the International Commission of Control.

The conditions of admission to the International are defined with some strictness. Every adherent party must bear the name of Communist, and in each country only one party can be recognised for the purpose of membership. The programme and the Statutes of that party and of the International must be accepted by all organisations which demand membership; and these must agree to abide by all the decisions of the party and the International. All members of parties must, in their turn, belong to organised groups in factory, or workshop, or mine, where they carry out the orders of their superiors. Discussion is free until a decision has been reached, but when this has been taken, it must be accepted by all members even if they disapprove of its substance.

The International, in fact, is built upon the basis of democratic centralisation; what that implies we shall discuss later. The World

Congress, of course, is at once too large and too occasional a body to be capable of effective leadership. It does, indeed, debate and pass resolutions; it also receives reports from its executive and the affiliated members. The Congress as it functions resembles the British Trade Union Congress more than any other body. It lives, that is to say, by trust in a number of leaders whom it chooses, and by providing them with a series of resolutions which indicate the categories within which they must work. Most of the reports it receives are documents too large in substance for effective debating in a big assembly; and the resolutions it accepts are much more the affirmation of wide principles the importance of which depends upon the method of their application. The Congress, in a word, is rather a great sounding board by which its executive learns the mood of the membership than a genuine legislative body. It indicates direction, but it cannot, from its very nature, control the movement in its passage along the road.

The effective leadership therefore belongs to the executive committee. This is a body the size of which does not appear to be constant, but has usually been some forty-five members. To the outside world, the executive committee has appeared essentially Russian in composition. In fact the Russians have only five members, the remainder being distributed among the national communist parties according to their size and importance; if the Russians appear to dominate the other members, that is, as Zinoviev has said, the result of their special experience, and the peculiar prestige which naturally attaches to Russian views in the movement as a whole. The executive directs the Communist International between the intervals of congresses. Its directions are binding upon affiliated organisations and control their activity. There is, indeed, an appeal from them to the World Congress, but this does not act to suspend any given direction. The executive, moreover, can exclude from the International, subject to an appeal thereto, any party, group, or member which attacks or weakens the programme and decisions of the World Congress. It possesses, again subject to appeal, the right to ratify the programmes of all affiliated bodies; and its decisions and official documents must be published in their journals by all sections of the latter. It has the right to send delegates to all local communist groups to explain its views, and these, like the representatives on mission during the French Revolution, can apply executive decisions even in the face of disagreement from the party concerned. The executive meets once in each month, and, where any questions of special importance arise, it may convoke a specially enlarged executive, at least twice each year, in which representatives of the affiliated organisations may take part.

Clearly, however, a committee of forty-five members is too large for detailed work. It can discuss generally, or, as the executive does, choose men for such tasks as editing the various publications of the International. But where so wide an area has to be covered, and where so much depends upon the assessment of value in minutiæ, it is essential that administrative work be entrusted to a small number. The executive therefore subdivides itself into two more or less permanent parts. Its præsidium is a specially selected group, of which the head is the chairman of the executive, directing the international work in the intervals of meetings of the executive. The bureau of organisation deals with all questions of organisation and finance, and appeal from its decisions lies only to the præsidium. There is also a secretary, elected by the executive, who, with his staff, forms a part of the bureau of organisation. Within these organs, certain special departments exist. The executive creates a special international secretariat to deal with the women's side of the movement; and it has sections which provide materials for information and statistics, agitation and propaganda, organisation and the very important Eastern Question. It retains also the right to create any special organs which experience suggests as advisable.

The best way, probably, to visualise the composition of the Communist International is to think of it in terms of English political institutions. The World Congress corresponds roughly to the House of Commons. It has the plenary authority which the latter in theory possesses, though, like the latter, it is, except on extraordinary occasions, guided and controlled by a body responsible nominally to itself. The executive corresponds to the Cabinet. While in theory it is carrying out the will of the Congress, as the Cabinet is carrying out the will of the House of Commons, in practice it shapes and determines that will by its superior coherency and driving power. The præsidium may be equated with the inner Cabinet; its members are the section to whom, by reason less of their titular position than the special authority attaching to their experience and capacity, guide and direct the others. The bureau of organisation is, with its secretarial branches, like a combination of the Cabinet secretariat and the Treasury.

The Congress, as was noted earlier, elects also an International Commission of Control. Its functions are four in number. It examines complaints against different sections of the executive and submits proposals for their remedy to the latter; it deals, secondly, with complaints referred to it by persons or parties against disciplinary measures taken against them, and once more submits proposals thereon to the executive; it controls, thirdly, the finances of the executive; and, finally, on the decision of the executive or its sections, it supervises the finances of the constituent parties of the International. The Commission, however, has no power to intervene in any internal party conflict, or in any dispute between the executive and a constituent party. Within its allotted field it is simply a bureau for the investigation of disputes and the submission of proposals, on the one hand, and the independent auditor of finance upon the other. It is not the master of the executive, but a servant with a quasi-independent right of ultimate access, by the proposals it formulates, to the World Congress.

As a piece of organisation, the International is clearly well thought out for the purposes it has in view. It is much more closely knit, and has a far more really coherent existence, than its rival, the Second International. The latter is merely a Congress with a non-executive secretariat; and it relies upon the action of national parties, themselves of loosely federal structure, to carry out such resolutions as it makes. The Second International, in fact, is not an effectively deciding body at all; it is much more an occasional conference with no means for continous action in its composition. A new European war might find it as inadequate for its announced purposes as was its predecessor in 1914. The Communist International, on the other hand, has the advantages of federation for the purposes of conference, with those of centralisation for the purposes of action. It has a general staff which infuses a consistent unity of thought and deed throughout its membership. The communist in the factory, the workshop, the local government party, the legislative assembly, each has his orders thought out in terms of a common need. The mechanisms have been created by means of which action can be planned and carried through as a whole. As an institutional system the Communist International resembles nothing so much as the Roman Catholic Church. There is the same width and intensity of discussion before dogma is imposed; there is the same authoritarian imposition of dogma; and there is the same ruthless purging of dissident elements which show unwillingness to accept the decisions made. The expulsion, for instance, of Ruth Fischer and the right-wing elements of German communism is remarkably similar in manner to the Roman treatment of the modernists. Dogma being laid down, delation of heresy follows; there is patient inquiry into details, the demand for proof before sentence, the offer of repentance and obedience to the accused. When, finally, recalcitrance is obvious, the sentence is carried out with exemplary severity, no matter what may be the previous services of those convicted.

The method has two obvious weaknesses. It tends, in the first place, to underestimate the need for flexibility in the movement. The executive, despite its body of reports, both written and personal, is not really in a position to issue orders for so far-flung a battle-line. The shades of national temper, the impact of national institutions, the thousand distracting counter-currents which make impossible any simple picture of a given situation, all tend to mislead the International; and the fact that it is *a priori* searching for the Marxian interpretation of some given position, leads it, too often, to apply formulæ to a situation which they merely misrepresent. Mistakes like the letter of Tomsky to the British Trade Unions in September, 1926, are the kind of price centralisation must pay. And the second weakness lies in the fact that the International tends to regard itself as the custodian of a doctrinal system from which diversions cannot be permitted. Anyone who studies, for instance, the answers given to the British Independent Labour Party in 1920, when the latter was seeking a *modus vivendi* with the Communist International, will realise that the latter is not unprepared to sacrifice power to orthodoxy. The mere *ipse dixit* of the International is not likely to persuade men to action who are dubious about its substance and remote from the atmosphere in which it appears as truth too obvious to need debate. Anyone, for example, who reads the discussion between the Second and Third Internationals in April 1922, in an effort to reach a basis of joint action, will be tempted to observe that it never occurred to the representatives of the latter to meet the minds of the Right Wing Socialists. They spoke, to use an ecclesiastical analogy once more, in much the same tone of authority that the Roman Church is accustomed to use towards the Anglican proponents of reunion; they had everything to receive, and nothing to give. They were prepared to surrender, but not for accommodation. Yet it was for accommodation that the conference had been called.

It may, in fact, be argued that the root error of the Communist International is a psychological one. It assumes that any diversity of view from its own is the proof of cowardice or crime in those who venture to differ. It applies uniform and equal solutions to things that are neither equal nor uniform. Its rejection of difference means that it comes ultimately to depend upon men whose interest it is less to analyse the facts about them objectively than to analyse them in such fashion as to make them square with a system of preconceived hypotheses. The effort, for instance, to read the problem of India in the set terms of Marxism is rather an exercise in ingenuity than a serious intellectual contribution to socialist advance. To treat the non-communist leaders of social democracy as necessarily blackguards and hypocrites, is, doubtless, convincing to communists; but it does not persuade those who have intimate acquaintance with those leaders that it is true. The communist policy of centralisation is admirably conceived for the purpose of creating disturbance; but it is too inflexible in its assumptions to make it likely that it is equally well conceived for the making of successful revolution. Its basis is too narrow, its dogmas too rigid, to give it the malleability of direction a world-movement requires.

It is, of course, true that the Communist International secures unswerving devotion from those who accept its authority. The courage of its exponents in every country where they have sought influence has been as remarkable as that of the Jesuit missionaries in the century after the formation of the order. But the basis upon which they seek to build is too narrow to win over those who fail to sympathise with their aims; and their attitude to the latter is unlikely to secure the unity of front which they preach to their adherents as essential to success. It is difficult to see why the leaders of the Second International should co-operate with them when the purpose of communists is to destroy their allies at the first opportunity. The ordinary socialist, indeed, tends as a consequence to look upon proffered communist assistance as insincere. It was noteworthy that in the British general strike of 1926 the communists played practically no part at all. Their alliance was rejected before it had been advanced simply because the leaders of the strike had made up their minds that it would be an alliance worked for ends with which they were not in sympathy. The net is spread vainly in sight of the bird. The allegiance of the communist to the orthodoxy of Moscow is so rigid and pre-eminent that other socialists regard it as incompatible with effective co-operation even for ends about which they are themselves eager.

That is perhaps brought out the more by a consideration of the programme, not of detail, but of principle, upon which the Communist International proceeds. It assumes that we are living in a period in which capitalism is making a frenzied effort to recover its domination. But the mind of labour is exacerbated against it, and its previous homogeneity has been lost as a result of problems, reparations, for example, created by the war. Capitalism, as a consequence, cannot rely upon the older methods; it halts between the uncertainty as to whether it should seek the immediate destruction of the revolutionary forces, or, by a policy of democracy, pacifism and petty reforms, seek the terms of survival along new lines. In the first case we have Fascism; in the second, governments like that of Branting or Ramsay Macdonald. The result of either is, however, disastrous to capitalism. The one obviously provokes revolution, the other, by its unreality, merely persuades the masses of the futility of representative government.

Revolution, then, remains inevitable from the communist standpoint, and the business of its adherents is to create great communist parties in each State to take advantage of the capitalist dilemma. The watchword of the Third World Congress, "Conquer communist influence in the majority of the working-class, and lead to the conflict the decisive part of this class" remains the key to events.

In this condition of unstable equilibrium, the obvious task of the International is to utilise the instability. If a Conservative government is in power, it must exacerbate the strife of class by fomenting and extending strikes. If a Labour government is in office, its adherents must make demands upon it of which the proletariat will approve, but which the capitalist cannot permit it to give. It must provoke suppressed nationalities to rise, and urge upon colonies the advantage of throwing off the yoke of the mother country. It must awaken the African and Asiatic races to revolt against their white exploiters. This situation of either constant, if sporadic conflict, or the instability of impending conflict, will prevent the capitalist from recovering the ground that he has lost. His difficulties will create proletarian discontent, the mood which an efficiently organised communist party will be able to utilise for revolutionary purposes.

Granted the truth of the original thesis upon which it is founded, the policy of the Communist International is certainly well conceived for the end it has in view. The only situation in which it is unlikely to make headway is one like that of America, where a wave of great natural prosperity makes men unwilling to risk the obvious gains of the present for the hazards of a dubious future. It is easy, for instance, to see that the unemployed of Great Britain might easily give ear to a doctrine which promises them, with audacious certainty, the prospect of ultimate reward. It is not difficult in a country like Greece to make the nationalist claim a part of a wider social movement. The Arab, the Chinaman, the African negro excluded from citizenship by prejudice and fear, will easily lend an ear to theories which insist upon the approaching end of the white man's exploitation. Wherever there exist suffering and injustice, there exists also a territory in which communism has reason to expect acceptance.

The difficulty of the view is, however, not less clear. It underestimates the difficulties it confronts and overestimates the possibilities of its success. It assumes, in the first place, that capitalism cannot check its propaganda. That is, to say the least, a dubious thing; certainly in Italy and in parts of the Near East, like Bulgaria and Roumania, the counter-offensive of capitalism has been proportionate to the vehemence of communist claims. It assumes, secondly, that the forces of social democracy can be persuaded to unite with its own army. Such evidence as there is indicates rather the untruth of this view. It suggests that, for at least a considerable period, the reformist parties of socialism will endeavour, in their own way, to march towards power. Whether if they attain it, they will use it wisely, it is, of course, impossible to say; but it is at least probable that not until their failure has been demonstrated will there supervene such a revolutionary mood as communists can utilise. Nor can it be said that their Eastern propaganda is likely to have the results they foresee. Undoubtedly it will exasperate the relations between East and West; but the destruction of Western influence does not necessarily mean communism. There is no special reason to suppose that the handful of Eastern intellectuals who frequent Moscow could, in a crisis, dominate India or China in the way, and with the purpose, of Lenin and Trotsky. It is much more logical, on the evidence, to admit that such propaganda would produce confusion. But what would be the outcome of that confusion no man save the boldest of prophets would venture to predict. Even if revolution came in the Western world, the prediction of victory is, after all, an hypothesis dependent upon mainly theoretical considerations. And the problem of its cost raises the not unimportant question of whether, in those terms, it could be regarded as a victory at all. The International is doubtless right in its insistence that men will not starve quietly under capitalism; but it is at least equally logical to argue that they are, similarly, unprepared to starve quietly under a proletarian dictatorship which cannot offer proof that the ideals of communism will ultimately triumph.

II

The difficulty, in fact, that the strategy of international communism presents does not lie either in some inherent wickedness in its ideals, or some clear likelihood that its immediate predictions will be falsified. It lies rather in the purely hypothetical character of its ultimate prophecies. Therein, it partakes less of the character of scientific probability than of religious certitude. Different as it is in appearance, it offers to its adherents much the same quality of prospect as Roman Catholicism or Mahomedanism. If the believer accepts its way of life, he can rest content in the assurance of an ultimate beatitude, with the difference that while the Churches can offer it to the individual, the communist can offer it only to some remote posterity. The faith, indeed, that he can arouse is not less intense than that of the religious enthusiast, but it is engendered at the expense of a scepticism in the face of social facts which few who note their uncertain complexity would be prepared to surrender. Faith, of course, is a powerful factor in enabling its possessors to put their dream to the proof. Yet, not seldom, the result of the test is disillusion instead of the expected confirmation.

Something of the same judgment will impose itself upon anyone who examines the strategy of communism within the confines of a national State. This appears to be built upon three assumptions. There must be built up, first, a strong communist party in each stage, firmly rooted, above all, in the trade-union movement. That party, in the second place, must co-operate with the social-democratic forces in order to convince the proletariat that representative institutions are worthless. It must, thirdly, establish an adequate influence over the peasantry in each State. Each of these aspects deserves separate consideration.

The building up of a strong communist party has been the subject of exhaustive discussion in the congresses of the International. The basis of this effort, it is argued, will be found in the individual workshops. Committees of communists must be formed in each in order that the trade-union movement may, through their influence, be increasingly orientated towards revolutionary action. Each of these committees or " cellules " must act as a party in little. It must examine all questions from the angle of party policy and act as a united whole. It must entrust a special function to each of its members, and hold him strictly to account for its performance. It must seek to enrol new members, and thus extend its influence. Since this "cellule" is the party's centre of gravity, too much importance cannot be attached to it. There must, moreover, be intimate connection between "cellules" in different enterprises, and special attention must be given to liaison with the Young Communist Party. The "cellule" must think of itself as an incipient soviet, ready, when the time comes, to assume quasi-governmental functions. It must regard itself as strictly subject to the orders of the party, and allegiance to the latter must supersede all other loyalties.

Special attention must be given to communist propaganda. "The party press," said the Second World Congress in 1920, "must be edited by reliable Communists who have proved their loyalty to the cause of the proletarian revolution. The dictatorship of the proletariat must not be spoken of as a mere hackneyed formula. The facts of everyday life must be systematically recorded and interpreted by the party press in such fashion as to make the necessity for proletarian dictatorship self-evident to every worker, soldier and peasant. All periodical and other publications of the party must be under the control of the central executive of the party, independently of whether the party is legal or illegal. Wherever the adherents of the Third International can gain access, and whatever means of propaganda are at their disposal, in the columns of the newspapers, at public meetings, within the Trade Unions and Co-operatives, it is essential that they denounce not only the capitalists, but also their allies, the reformists of every shade and colour." The party, moreover, must think out such educational institutions as will provide at least an elementary knowledge of communist principles for all its members. In the evenings and on Sundays it must organise schools and lectures, while for those with some instruction in communism it must attempt more advanced and systematic instruction. Its purpose, in this educational effort, must be to train qualified militants who can serve as party propagandists. Attention, also, must be paid to non-communist institutions like popular universities and labour colleges which can be influenced in a communist direction. Circles for the study of communism should be created, especially for the youth of the party, and an adequate literature, particularly of the works of Marx and Lenin, should be made available. Steps should be taken to bring all such educational institutions into contact, by the intermediary of the International, with similar bodies in Moscow. Above all, it is essential to put an end to the isolation and independence of communist students who should, by appropriate direction, be organised to serve in, and take part in the practical work of, the party without exception.[1]

Propaganda, however, must go further. " Every organisation desiring to join the Communist International," resolved the Second World Congress, " must be bound systematically and regularly to remove from all responsible positions (in the party, committee, editorial staff, trade union, parliamentary group, co-operative society, and municipal council) all reformists and supporters of the 'centre' and to replace them by tried communists, even at the risk of supplanting, for a time, 'experienced' men by rank and file workmen." It is in accordance with this resolution that the British Communist Party[2] instructs its members to get elected where possible to important conferences of the Labour Party (from which communists have been expelled) and to act within their ranks upon the instructions of their own headquarters. They are to inform the latter of all resolutions at such conferences, to act there as an organised delegation, and to form secret communist "fractions" in Labour parties, trade unions and similar bodies. They are to report back upon their activity in this matter, and to

[1] The reader will find a most interesting discussion of communist propaganda and education in the resolutions of the Fifth World Congress (French edition, pp. 46–56).

[2] Bulletin of June 24th, 1926.

realise, in the words of the British representative upon the Executive of the International, "that in whatever capacity our Party members are serving in the general working-class movement, their party allegiance must supersede all other responsibilities."

Nor must their propaganda stop there. The heart of the modern State, and the main defence of capitalism, lies in its armed forces. It is therefore essential to penetrate into its ranks by a systematic and persistent campaign. Where this is prohibited by law, it must be done despite the law. "Refusal to carry on or participate in such work," says the World Congress, "should be considered as treason to the revolutionary cause and incompatible with membership of the Third International." It was, of course, in accordance with these instructions that the British Communist Party addressed its appeal to the troops not to shoot down strikers which resulted in the imprisonment of its leaders after the famous trial of 1925. And the communist, from his angle, is clearly right in his emphasis upon this aspect of his work. "No great revolution has happened, or can happen," wrote Lenin, "without the disorganisation of the army. . . . The new social class which aspires to power has never been able and is even to-day unable, to assure and maintain its authority without the complete dislocation of the old army." The communist, moreover, argues that this is a less difficult task than might appear. For not only are the majority of soldiers and sailors themselves drawn from the proletariat, they also dislike intensely being used in civil disturbances. Intensified propaganda in a period of revolutionary crisis may, by operating upon these impulses, go far to neutralise the influence of the government upon the troops. That is especially the case when they are themselves discontented; and it is an integral point of communist propaganda not only to promote fraternisation with soldiers and sailors, but also to put themselves behind every grievance of a proletarian character these may announce. Historically, moreover, it is important to remember that at revolutionary periods it has not always been possible to rely upon the troops—Cromwell had difficulty with them in his persecution of Lilburne and the Levellers; revolutionists were able to exploit the grievances of the sailors in the mutiny of 1797; in 1789 the citizens of Paris were able to infect the French troops with their own revolutionary enthusiasm; in the attack upon the communists in 1871 many of the troops refused to fire; and it was the propaganda among the Russian army by the Bolsheviks which secured their triumph in 1917. It must, moreover, be remembered that one of the conditions of a successful use of the army in a dispute is its confinement to a single area; if the outbreak is widespread, the power of authority is greatly minimised. "A decentralised army," writes Mr. William Paul,[1] "during an intense industrial upheaval, is easily approached and disaffected." Clearly, also, the use of troops to quell civil disturbance would be gravely compromised if there was organised resistance to their movement by railroad and transport workers. Communists build largely upon the hope which, to an outsider may appear faint indeed, that, in a period of excitement, they will be able to pervert the loyalty of troops so that the latter will refuse to fire.

Upon one other feature of this aspect of the communist position it is necessary to say a word. It is integral to their conception of necessary strategy that every effort should be made to discredit reformist leaders. This attitude goes back to Marx himself, who advised its adoption in the period when it was necessary for communists to dissociate themselves from the right-wing socialists. It is emphasised in every communist publication. They are stigmatised as hypocrites, traitors, lacqueys, according to the mood of the moment. In the single small volume of Lenin on the *State and Revolution* Paltchinski is charged with corruption, Tchernoff and Tseretelli with being "allies of the millionaire thieves who plunder the public treasury," or "the heroes of putrid philistinism"; Plek-

[1] *Communism and Society*, p. 182. Mr. Paul's book is easily the ablest English exposition of the communist position.

hanoff, from 1908 to 1917, with being " half doctrinaire and half philistine, walking, politically, in the wake of the bourgeoisie " ; Bernstein is a " renegade," and the whole English Labour Party is indistinguishable from " lower middle-class democrats." Communists have a special genius for general invective on, it appears, the principle that if enough mud is thrown, some is bound to stick. They cannot believe in the sincerity of socialists who do not accept their own views; and they hold themselves bound to do all in their power to prevent others from accepting them as sincere.

It is, then, a little curious to discover the emphasis they place upon the tactic of the united front. Nothing shows more strikingly the flexibility of the Communist International than the power of its leaders to impose this view upon their followers. They had preached so long the infamy of the reformist leaders that many of their most devoted adherents were horrified at the thought of collaborating with them. It was pointed out that the left wing of the movement would be estranged by a policy which savoured of dubious compromise, and that the revolutionary zeal of many might easily be tainted by association with men who detested that outlook. To Lenin and his colleagues, however, such a view was untenable. In the early days of the Russian Revolution, when they expected a world-revolution immediately, non-collaboration seemed essential.

But the moment for a world-revolution had gone by. The years of war had tired the masses, and they sought, above all things, a period of quiescence. That period endangered the strength of communism since it was evident to the workers that the communists everywhere promoted schism, and, by dividing the proletarian forces, strengthened the hands of the capitalist. The socialists of the right were therefore able to represent their revolutionary critics as the fomenters of dissension in the face of the enemy. They were themselves trusted by millions of working-men, and it was folly to take no account of that trust. On the contrary, it was necessary to destroy it, and that could be only by boring from within a movement to which, in essence, communists were opposed.

Complete separation from the reformist forces therefore received short shrift from the Third International; to insist upon it was, in Lenin's phrase, the "infantile malady of communism." It became the accepted policy to force upon the Right separation from the bourgeois parties, and the endeavour was made to secure terms of collaboration from those whom communists had attacked. The result, in the communist view, would be that the workers would throw the liability for defeat upon the Right if the manœuvre was rejected; while if it was accepted, since communists would not surrender their freedom to agitate and act in their own fashion, they would be provided with an incomparable platform. To support the Right did not imply to strengthen them; "I support Henderson by my vote," said Lenin, "as the rope supports a man who is being hanged." To support the Right meant to separate the working-class from the bourgeoisie, and to force upon the former a programme which pushes its leaders continually towards more revolutionary principles. It means the formulation of demands which appear just to the workers but impossible to the capitalists; it defines, accordingly, the class-character of the differences between them. Their refusal insists upon the necessity of conflict, and conflict means the passage of leadership over to the communists. The more unified, in short, the working-class becomes, the nearer it moves to power; and even those workers who see nothing communist in united action will find, when they are engaged in it, that they have been pursuing a communist policy without knowing it. They will have had contact of an intimate kind with revolutionists and the creed of revolution which cannot but serve the end that communism has in view. What is proposed is not a union of parties but a limited collaboration which will force the right wing of socialism into the revolutionary path.

The tactic of the united front is, then, a Machiavellian manœuvre dictated by the necessities of the international situation; it is the policy which the French socialist, Longuet, not inaptly described in the famous line of Racine: "I embrace my rival, but it is the better to choke him." Since the policy was first adumbrated, in 1920, it cannot be said to have progressed rapidly. Most of the right-wing parties have refused, in England by enormous majorities, to admit the communists within their ranks; and the Second International in 1926, rejected by 247 votes to 3 a proposal of the Independent Labour Party of Great Britain for a joint conference with the Third International "to explore the possibilities of the formation of an all-inclusive International." Communists have therefore, as in Great Britain, been compelled to fall back upon expedients such as the formation of special conferences and minority movements to maintain contact with the right wing of Socialism.

But it cannot by any means be said that the strategy has been a failure. An appeal from Russia, in the first place, naturally exercises an immense psychological influence upon working-class mentality; its rejection even causes discussion, and that, in itself, is a stimulus to the understanding of communism. The workers, moreover, as the communists quite rightly see, are sick to death of the endless schisms in the ranks of socialism. They realise that the communists are among the most energetic and ardent of themselves; and there are many who resent their exclusion from the movement as a wasteful handicap. That attitude, moreover, is intensified, whenever the forces of capitalism secure a victory over labour. Division in the labour ranks is always a contributory cause of defeat; and the emotional satisfaction of closing up the ranks cannot easily be estimated. The antagonism to the communists, moreover, is certainly stronger among the leaders and officials of the right wing than it is among the rank and file. The weakness of the communists' case lies, of course, in two directions. They have, firstly, too obviously insisted upon the fact that by co-operation they do not mean co-operation. The eager party man in the social democratic ranks resents the proffer of aid which is avowedly given with the tongue in the cheek. And, secondly, he finds collaboration difficult with men who have treated a social democratic State like Georgia in the same high-handed fashion as France treated the Ruhr or Poland Lithuania; while the continued imprisonment and oppression of socialists in Soviet Russia not unnaturally makes him suspicious of suggested collaboration elsewhere. The general sense of social democrats seems to be that the communists are "too clever" and that no association with them could possibly be sincere.

That does not mean that association may not be forced upon the right wing. The communists, after all, are a working-class party. They predict that reforms are impossible within the ambit of capitalism. If, over a period, there is a general worsening of the standards of labour, the demand for collaboration will inevitably grow simply because their insight will have seemed superior. And any effort at prosecution, as in the British trials of 1925, and in the aftermath of the general strike of 1926, will, they believe, have the same effect. Nothing makes more for sympathy than martyrdom in a cause akin to one's own. Attempts by governments to suppress communism only compel the rest of the socialist movement to defend its adherents in the name of freedom; and such defence, on any united scale, would necessarily lead at least to some loose form of united action. Nor must one omit the other side. Few English miners are likely in this generation to forget that in their struggle against the owners and the British Government in 1926 they received aid from Russian trade unions upon a scale unprecedented in labour history. The gift may not have been without ulterior motives. But what impresses men in their hour of trial is the fact rather than the sources of aid. The generosity of Russia to the miners is not unlikely to create in the latter the sense that, whatever the difference of outlook, the ultimate community of interest has been solidly demonstrated. That is an important prospect; for it is unnecessary to dwell upon the pivotal position the miners occupy in the British Labour movement.

The problem of the peasantry has always played a special part in the strategy of communism; from the time of Engels' book on the agrarian question it has been realised that special attention must be given to the need for enlisting his support. " The proletariat," resolved the Fifth World Congress of the International, " can neither conquer power, nor build the Soviet régime, unless it has, over a long period, sought to neutralise certain elements of the peasant class, and win the sympathy of others. . . . Communist parties which have not been able to organise revolutionary action among the peasants cannot be recognised as mass-parties seriously aiming at power."

That emphasis is a very natural one in the light of the history of the Russian Revolution. For what was a primary cause of the Bolshevik victory was the insistence of the party, and especially of Lenin, that the land must be given to the peasants. The Cadets, in their brief period of power, gave no attention to the problem of the land; while the Kerensky régime was so hesitant that peasant revolts broke out all over Russia, and the government sought to repress them by military force.

Lenin was quick to see that this was the turning-point in the revolution. " A peasant rebellion in an agrarian country," he wrote, " against the government of the socialist—revolutionary Kerensky, of the Mensheviks, and of other ministers representing the interests of capital and of the landed seigneurs ! A repression of this rebellion by a republican government by means of revolutionary force ! In the face of such facts, can any partisan of the proletariat deny that the crisis is about to burst forth, that the revolution is at a decisive turning-point, that the victory of the government over the peasant rebellion now would sound the knell of the revolution ? "

Into the brilliant use of this position by the Bolsheviks to manipulate their own victory, it is not possible here to enter; nor can we discuss the effort of the communists, when in power, to control the peasant power they had brought into being. It must suffice to point out, first, that they discovered that the resistance of the peasants to a policy of socialisation is insurmountable. And, secondly, that the absence of a communist mentality among the poorer peasantry makes it impossible, save over a period too long to contemplate, to bring the rural districts into the categories of the communist society.[1]

[1] This is admirably brought out in the second part of Mr. Michael Farbman's *After Lenin* (1925), which gives an excellent résumé of the history of the peasant question.

It is probably this experience which explains the agrarian policy of the International. It seeks for an alliance between the poorer peasantry and the working-class. So long, it argues, as the former are dominated by the large landowners and their agents, a victory is impossible. Communists should therefore seek to drive a wedge between the peasant organisations and the rich agrarian class. They should assist, by all means in their power, the claims of the poorer peasants. They should demand the expropriation of all large estates and their free distribution to the peasantry. They should incite the small farmer to fight for the reduction of taxes, and even their abolition, while the taxation of the large farmer is rigorously insisted upon. In season and out of season, they should endeavour to show the peasant that their demands can only secure full satisfaction by a policy of confiscating the large estates. They should support all agrarian strikes, and preach incessantly the solidarity of interest between the worker without capital and the peasant without land. By thus driving a wedge between the rich and poor peasants, by bringing it home to the latter that the class-structure of society has the same results in agriculture as in industry, there can be formed a block of peasants and workers which will be of vital import when the day of reckoning comes.

How far this strategy is realistic it is impossible to say. Certainly in Russia itself, the working of the thesis laid down by Lenin in his proposed " Platform for the Proletarian Party," has been only very partially applied; and its results are not in accord with communist expectations. Indeed there is much to be said for the view that because communism itself is a theory evolved from the conditions of industry, it does not apply, even with the modifications upon which Lenin insisted, to the mentality which operates in agrarian life. The peasant is interested in revolution up to the point where he obtains the land. Once he has got it, and can work it, the aftermath of revolution does not seem to win his interest. It is probable, accordingly, that communist agitation might go far towards winning the support of the poorer peasants against any system which either divorces them from security of tenure or treats them oppressively. That was true in the agrarian revolution in England in the sixteenth century; it was true, also, of France in 1789; and it was demonstrated once more by Russian experience in 1917. But whether, having won the soil, the peasant can be induced to pool his interests with those of the townsman, is a question upon which we have no real knowledge except the empirical fact that no amount of force will induce him to do so. For his answer to force is the effective one of diminishing cultivation, and the townsman is compelled to surrender in order that he may get food. No social class has the same unending power to wait that the peasant possesses. His proximity to Nature breeds an endurance different in kind from every other class in society.

To the communists, the problem of nationality is a part of the general problem of imperialism. The latter system being a method whereby capitalism retains its power over the masses, it is essential to free the national groups which seek autonomy from their bondage. "All colonies and subject territories," writes Stalin, "have the right to separate completely from the State with which they are connected, and to form an independent State; in the same way the possibility of territorial annexations is ruled out." So Macedonia and Thrace ought to be aided by communists in their effort towards independence; the Serbs, Croats, and Slovenes ought to be disunited into separate republics; and the Lithuanian population of Poland should have the right to self-determination. For so long as the national question remains, a barrier stands in the way of unity between the proletariat of different countries; and this issue is exploited by the bourgeoisie to the detriment of the revolution. Obviously, for example, so long as the Irish worker was depressed by his subjection to the British people, he could not give adequate attention to the essential, that is, the economic, situation; remove the first issue, and the true problem will assert itself. So, also, with the exploitation of India by Great Britain. It is futile to believe that a hold can be obtained there for communist propaganda unless it is built upon sympathy with the Indian demand for self-determination. Aid for that movement serves a double purpose. On the one hand, it weakens British imperialism in a vital spot, and, on the other, it brings communist propagandists into contact with the discontented by support of whom they are able to find a place for their own views.

"The bourgeoisie in each country," writes Bukharin, "exploits and oppresses the proletariat of its own land. But it does its utmost to convince its own proletariat that the latter's enemies are not to be found among bourgeois fellow-countrymen, but among the peoples of other lands. The aim of this is to switch off the class-struggle of the workers against their capitalist oppressors into a struggle between nationalities." To support, accordingly, the movement for self-determination is to oppose a serious barrier to the safety of capitalism and to help the working-class of an oppressed country to maintain sympathy even for the working-class of the country by which they are oppressed. For when they realise that the workers sympathise with their demand for freedom, and that it is the master-class which opposes it, they will see that their struggle against national oppression is only a form of the struggle against capitalist oppression. They will be ripe for the reception of communist ideas, willing to join with the workers of other lands for deliverance from a common yoke. National self-determination, in fact, is a stage in the development of international working-class solidarity. And the same argument applies, *mutatis mutandis*, to the problem of oppression in creed or colour or race. Take anti-semitism, for example. "The Russian bourgeoisie," writes Bukharin, "raised the hunt against the Jews not only in the hope of diverting the anger of the exploited workers, but also in the hope of freeing themselves from competitors in commerce and industry. . . . Anti-semitism is one of the forms of resistance to socialism."

The rise of communism has coincided with an intense growth of national and racial feeling all over the world. The Peace of Versailles put an end to many national oppressions, but it created almost as many as it destroyed. The position of Japan in world-politics, moreover, the growth of national feeling in China, the plea for self-determination by Indian and Filipino, these, and things like these, have combined to give an importance to the communist thesis which cannot be gainsaid. Wherever a national minority feels itself outraged, there will be found a seed-ground for communist propaganda; and wherever there is exploitation of race by race—as in Africa, for example—it is easy to see that communist insistence on racial equality provides an impetus to accept its coincident hypotheses. That it should have made progress, accordingly, in India and China, and, more slowly, in the Near East is not remarkable; and, in the Near East, a White Terror has been sufficiently general to make communism the antithesis it is natural for opponents to accept. Strategically, therefore, it is very difficult to doubt that the weapon evolved has been used by communists with great skill. And no one who reads the record of such bodies as their Far Eastern Congress, can doubt either that they are great dramatic artists who know how to exploit to the full the situations they discover.

But it is necessary to distinguish between the communist strategy of self-determination and the theory and practice of that principle. Georgia, for example, was a Menshevik community, and the Soviet Government overran it, partly for military, and partly for economic purposes, exactly as a capitalist government might have done. The reasons advanced for so doing have at least the merit of simplicity. " We do not only recognise," wrote Trotsky,[1] " but we give full support to,

[1] *Daily Herald*, April 3rd, 1922.

the principle of self-determination, whenever it is directed against feudal, capitalist and imperialist States. But wherever the fiction of self-determination becomes, in the hands of the bourgeoisie, a weapon directed against the proletarian revolution (as in the case of Georgia), we have no occasion to treat this fiction differently from the other 'democratic principles' perverted by capitalism." The principle, in fact, is a tactic, and it must be applied only in relation to other principles which may countermand its application. It is, moreover, obvious that the communists gravely overestimate the economic factor in nationalism. True though it is that nationalism may be exploited by governments for economic purposes, it is yet also true that the consciousness of a separate existence implied by nationalism would have to receive recognition in the business of government even if a world-revolution everywhere enthroned communism in power. For that consciousness, with all it implied, existed long before industrialism had effected the class-division against which communism is a protest. The removal of economic injustice would, doubtless, largely mitigate its intensity; but there would remain problems of language, culture, religion, which would not easily yield to international control. Since, moreover, the international character of communism is very largely the response to the international character of capitalism, the interesting question arises whether the destruction of the latter would leave communism its international character. There would still be the problem of raw materials and their disposition, and an inability on the part of a World Soviet to agree with a Russian Soviet about the use of the oil deposits in Caucasia might easily lead to intense conflict in which the Russian sense of nationalism would be passionately aroused. And, in any case, it is obvious that a civilisation like our own could not exist (as Trotsky has seen) if self-determination were carried out whenever any national group happened to want it. No one need doubt the value of local autonomy; but no one, either, can doubt that the habit of the small nation to push its demands into the region of sovereign statehood has been little less than a disaster to the world.[1]

III

One of the main problems by which any party is confronted is the question of the limits within which it exacts obedience from its members to the programme it has formulated. It exists, in the phrase of Burke, to promote a body of principles upon which its members are agreed. But, obviously, enough, some measure of divergence must be permitted. In the Roman Catholic Church,

[1] Cf. my *Grammar of Politics*, Chap. VI.

which is probably the most centralised organisation in the world, there are many matters upon which members may take a divergent view. The Conservative Party in England contains people with views so different from one another as those of the Duke of Northumberland and Lord Henry Bentinck. The Liberal Party contains extreme individualists at one end and collectivists at the other. The Labour Party contains monarchists and republicans, men who, like Mr. J. H. Thomas, believe profoundly in the British Empire, and others, like Mr. Bertrand Russell, who disbelieve emphatically in the assumption that it has a mission. The Church of England is divisible into Broad Church, Evangelical, and Catholic parties. The Republican party in America contained strong advocates of governmental control and equally strong believers that industrial regulation was no concern of government. In general, clearly, the average organisation draws fairly widely the limits of orthodoxy; for expulsion for heresy, as distinct from self-expulsion, is one of the rarest occurrences in modern times.

The communist theory of party discipline is built upon quite different assumptions; its theory of discipline seems midway between that of an army and the Roman Catholic Church. Like the latter, it has a body of doctrine, the teaching of Marx and Lenin, which indicates the broad dogmas, the class-war, the dictatorship of the proletariat and the like, which its members must hold. Upon the application of doctrine to any given position, differences and discussion are permitted until a decision has been taken; but, after that has been done, an absolute and loyal obedience from those who dissent therefrom is expected. As in an army, that is to say, even the commander who doubts the wisdom of attack must carry it out exactly as though he was convinced of its rightness. There cannot be conflict of direction, nor, once the decision has been made, can there be permitted attacks upon, or groups to reverse, that decision. The party has been everywhere rigorously consistent in imposing these limitations upon its members. It has carried out "purgings" of the party; members whose enthusiasm has not been proved in action have been dropped from its ranks. It has expelled men like Paul Levi in Germany for doubting the tactics of the united front. Zinoviev and Trotsky have been penalised equally with the humblest members. Warnings and exhortations have been addressed even to the authors of articles in the party press which might be suspected of lukewarmness to the official policy. There cannot, it is argued, be a united strategy against capitalism if every group of dissenters is to form a faction for the propagation of its own ideas. The Communist Party is the general staff of the proletariat; if its members remained free to obey or disobey its orders at will, it would soon degenerate into a mere debating society. Hence the elaborate provisions in the statutes of the Communist International for the enforcement of discipline and the punishment of disobedience.[1]

It should be emphasised that the imposition of penalties does not prevent the most vivid discussion before a policy is adopted. Theses, reports, programmes, speeches, are accumulated upon one another almost to the point of exhaustion; it does not appear that, prior to defeat, any defeated group can claim that it has not had its day in court. Internationally, moreover, there is a system of appeals to the World Congress which gives it, even when the decision has been applied, the right to attempt its reversal by discussion. And one of the outstanding features of the system is the large part taken by the leaders themselves in meeting and making attacks. An Englishman would be astonished if Mr. Baldwin or Lord Oxford went to a party conference for the purpose of taking an intimate and daily part in its proceedings; but Lenin, Trotsky, Zinoviev, Clara Zetkin, Radek, do so as a matter of course. It is, indeed, remarkable to note, in the record both of national and international congresses, the care with which

[1] Reprinted in the *Proceedings* of the Fifth World Congress (French Edition, p. 38 f.).

preparation has been made to deal with criticism and attack. To some extent, perhaps, the British Labour Party's Annual Conference displays a similar situation, but its proceedings reveal, not seldom, an effort by the machine to repress the discussion of inconvenient questions very different from the boldness with which they are faced in Communist Congresses.

The advantage of the method is, of course, obvious. It enables every member of the party to know what he is to believe, and its directors to tell him, with the sanction of ultimate penalties at their disposal, what he is to do. For the purpose of the offensive in attack, this is a great merit. For the average member of the party, it probably dispenses with the problems of conscience in much the same way as an *ex cathedra* pronouncement from Rome controls the attitude of its adherents. Its weaknesses, however, are not less manifest. Few able men, whose advice has been rejected, are able to carry out a policy in which they disbelieve. In this respect, the analogy of an army breaks down; for there is no real comparison between, say, an order to a commander to attack a trench and an order to an English or French communist to pursue the policy of a united front. It may, moreover, be doubted whether the loyalty produced by the system is as real as it is apparent; certainly, at least since the death of Lenin, the factionalism it is supposed to suppress seems rather to be driven underground than to disappear. If suppression is thoroughgoing, it deprives the party of those whose sincerity prevents them from offering an artificial conformity; while if it is inadequate, it is absurd.

Nor is that all. Thought cannot, in any system, be destroyed by penalties, even if it can be hampered; the roots of loyalty are internal and not external. The system attempts to impose an intellectual dictatorship in the one region of effort where dictatorships are invariably, if ultimately only, unsuccessful. And it seems, further, to have the great demerit of hampering the work of thought in the party. A French communist, for instance, who is convinced that the united front is an erroneous strategy does not fight the executive of the International on equal terms. It would be factionalism on his part to discuss it in the press in order to obtain a decision on his behalf; and a single debate at an annual or biennial congress, in which he can make a long speech to a congress inevitably dominated by the executive—which, by definition, is committed to an alternative view—does not give him any great opportunity of producing conviction; and this, in its turn, assumes that he would be allowed by the national party to go to Moscow with such an intention. Communists are not less skilful than other parties in the art of manipulating delegations.

It is therefore probable that this theory of party discipline produces an artificial uniformity purchased at the expense of intellectual creativeness; and this, it may be suggested, is borne out by a certain heavy inflexibility in communist literature—such masters of the controversial art as Lenin and Trotsky being exceptions—which makes it too often palatable to the reader who already accepts communism than to the one who is still awaiting conversion. It has, moreover, one other weakness. On the one hand, it insists that victory can only be won by iron discipline within its own ranks; on the other, it asks for a united front with men from whose doctrines and methods it avowedly disagrees. It announces that the primary loyalty of its own members is, on pain of exclusion, to the orders of the Communist International; within that body it prohibits any sort of faction. Yet it urges its members, as in England, to enter the Labour Party, the trade unions, the trade councils, the organised unemployed, and there to form factions for the purpose of weakening the authority of the accepted programme. Quite intelligibly and logically the Labour Party looks with suspicion on proffers of alliance from communists on the ground that they propose to do within its ranks what they would not permit within their own. Their policy, in brief, of an allegiance which does not admit of open-minded co-operation with alternative views, naturally promotes distrust of the very united front they hope to secure. And any action they take to promote a rigorous obedience in their own ranks only strengthens that mistrust by emphasising the dubious sincerity of the co-operation they offer.

IV

Upon one final question a word should be said. Because communism is a doctrine of revolution, its adherents are often attacked, especially for tactical reasons, on the ground that they are anxious, at any possible moment, to make an attack upon the established order. That is not, of course, the case. There have been revolutionists, notably the Frenchman, Blanqui, of whom this could be said with truth; but of the modern communists, and above all, of Lenin, it is grotesquely erroneous. They take their stand by the classic words of Marx that insurrection is an art, and they are anxious that it should not be practised save under promising conditions. Marx himself, as is well known, was opposed to the Commune in 1871; and the defence of it was built upon admiration of its courage rather than recognition of its timeliness. So also, the communists of our own time considered the Hamburg insurrection of 1922 a mistake. Time and conditions were unsuitable and that unsuitability is a grave error because it compromises the future.

What, then, are the conditions of strategic success? "Armed insurrection," wrote Lenin, "is a special form of political struggle. It is subject to special rules which must be deeply reflected upon"; and Trotsky, in a most suggestive analysis of the Revolution of October,[1] has explained the need for a careful study of revolutionary insurrection and the construction of a code of rules out of the lessons implicit therein. From a study of Marx, Lenin lays down five rules as the guiding principles of the act. It is important, firstly, never to play with insurrection; once it has commenced, it must be carried through to the bitter end. When, secondly, the revolutionists have chosen the decisive time and place, they must mass there forces superior to those of the enemy; otherwise, the latter, being better prepared and organised, will destroy them. Having begun, in the third place, it is essential to act with determination and, whatever the price, to assume the offensive; "the defensive," said Marx, "is death to the insurrection." The element of

[1] See his most suggestive pamphlet *The Lessons of October*, 1917 (English translation by A. Susan Lawrence, 1925).

surprise is, fourthly, fundamental; and the moment must always be seized when the forces of your opponent are scattered. Keep, finally, whatever happens, moral superiority; successes must be won daily and even hourly, if the theatre of war is small. That depresses your opponent and consolidates your power of keeping the offensive. Above all, each of these maxims must be read in the background of Danton's great phrase, "*L'audace, encore l'audace, et toujours l'audace!*" [1]

Such rules, of course, are general in character; and it will be helpful to supplement them by certain lessons impressed by experience. It is essential to smash the machinery of the State that is assaulted; revolutionists must not repeat the mistake of Louis Blanc in 1848 and accept institutions devised for a non-revolutionary purpose and functioning as such. Only new institutions will confer proper and full initiative upon the revolutionists. In the civil war that revolution provokes, moreover, the communists should "fearlessly display their final objective before the people." They can be certain that in so doing they will win support; they can be certain also, if the degree of class-consciousness in the masses be adequate, that the bourgeoisie will, in this aspect, have difficulty in rivalling them. It must be remembered,

[1] Lenin, *On the Road to Insurrection* (English translation, 1926), p. 112.

further, that revolution is a drastic educator; to begin an insurrection successfully is to attract waverers, the *petite bourgeoisie* for instance, and to free the poorer peasantry from bourgeois influence by showing them that alliance with you is the direct road to the realisation of their own demands. Moreover, to show unshakeable decision oneself is a factor in transforming the natural inertia of the masses into active sympathy; it transforms their complaints into demands. On the other hand, to hesitate when the moment has come, is to create vacillation not only amongst one's followers, but among the masses also, and thus to destroy the opportunity. It is important to remember that the act of insurrection itself creates confusion and anxiety everywhere. The workers are undecided and your opponents do not know what is in your mind. Your possession of the initiative, because you know your own mind, is the secret of your striking power.

Neither Lenin nor his followers conceal from themselves the difficulty of estimating whether the assumption that the hour has struck is accurate. It is well known, for instance, that from April until October 1917, Lenin stood almost alone in insisting that the Bolsheviks must rise against the Kerensky Government; even followers so eminent as Zinoviev and Kamenev were passionately convinced of his error. But, for Lenin, the conditions of October fulfilled the hypothesis upon which, in his view, the success of any effort depended. "In order to be entirely victorious," he wrote, early in September 1917, "insurrection must not depend on a conspiracy, or a party, but on a revolutionary class. That is the first point. Insurrection must depend on the revolutionary pressure of all the people. That is the second point. Insurrection must break out at the apogee of the rising revolution, that is, at the moment when the activity of the vanguard of the people is greatest, when fluctuations among the enemy *and among the weak and indecisive friends of the revolution are strongest.* That is the third point. It is in bringing these three conditions to the consideration of the question of insurrection that Marxism differs from Leninism."[1]

Roughly speaking, it is clear that, in this analysis, the conditions of a successful revolution reduce themselves to three: there must be a revolutionary class-consciousness, there must be a strong communist party to take advantage of that situation, and it must, in its turn, be directed by leaders who have the courage to will, the eye to see, and the resource to manœuvre. These assumptions are extraordinarily interesting, but their very character indicates the problems to which

[1] *On the Road to Insurrection,* p. 57. The letter, which is an extraordinarily brilliant analysis, should be read in its entirety.

they give rise. It is clear, in the first place, that they are an admirable summary of the Russian situation. There the machine of government had broken down; the angry masses were making demands the Government could not satisfy; the Bolsheviks proclaimed with the vigour of a concentrated and trained band their willingness to satisfy those demands; they seized the initiative and never lost it through the division and bewilderment of their opponents; and they had in Lenin—on any showing one of the supreme political strategists of modern history—the ideal leader for the situation.

But the real inference from this experience is that such strategy will only be successful in a kindred environment. The essential fact is that, in Russia in 1917, two parties confronted each other, both of them minority parties, and that one only had the insight to voice the aspirations of the people. The success of Lenin, in other words, was built on the fact that the purposes he embodied for the people were the purposes the people themselves passionately desired. He won because public opinion supported him. And, in such an environment, any strong party that is greatly led will win. If a bourgeois government outrages the people; if, in the midst of unsuccessful war, the army becomes mutinous, if a communist party, at that moment and under an inspired leader, passionately pledges itself to redress the outrage; then it is likely to repeat the victory of 1917. Yet the lesson of October is also a warning not less than an example. The inspired leader is rare; Lenin, and to some extent, Trotsky, had to dominate their party as few parties will agree to be dominated. Few governments are as outrageous as that of Tsarist Russia or as confused and incompetent as that of Kerensky. Few armies are likely to suffer such disorganisation and ill-treatment as the Russian Army during the European War of 1914. And if communists can learn how to organise revolution from experience, from the same experience bourgeois governments can also learn how to organise against it. "Political ends," as Lord Morley wrote, "miscarry, and the revolutionary leader treads a path of fire." The adventure is dubious in any event, and, in most conceivable instances, it is so hazardous that it can hardly hope to overcome its difficulties.

It is not argued here that the Marxian view of the insurrectionary art is incorrect; on the contrary, it is suggested that its substance is entirely accurate. But it is suggested that the environment for which it is suitable is of extreme rarity in history; and that even when such an environment is afforded, only a supreme genius will be able to take advantage of it. The lesson it teaches is, indeed, the lesson which all governments must learn on pain of ceasing to be governments: that no authority can resist deeply felt and widespread demands from the people. If they do, it is not improbable that an attempt will be made to give substance to the communist theory of insurrection, and, under adequate leadership, it might well succeed. An English government, for example, that sought to reduce trade unions to impotence; a French government which attempted to reconstitute the monarchy; these might easily reproduce a situation in which the Marxian strategy would be successful. But either government, in this view, would by its attitude have revealed its complete lack of any sense of values, and it would have amply deserved its fate. Nor must it be forgotten that the lessons of the Russian Revolution are not merely applicable in communist terms. The dictatorship of Mussolini is merely their transference to the service of the bourgeoisie; and they indicate the important truth that once the floodgates are opened, none can surely prophesy who will emerge from the disaster as leader. That is the risk men run when they desert the path of reason and choose to prove for themselves by force not their desire for truth, but the truth of their desires. There are occasions, doubtless, when the situation they confront leaves them no alternative save violent protest. But its conscious choice as the path of salvation seems likely, save in the most rare of instances, to lead to disillusion rather than to success.

CONCLUSION

NOTHING is gained, in any discussion of communism, by treating it as a wicked doctrine which would never have arisen if a handful of criminal adventurers had not devoted themselves to its propagation. Like any other system of belief, its rise is the outcome of its environment, and its acceptance by large bodies of men is no more unnatural than their acceptance of other creeds. Those to whom it appears either wicked or impossible, too impotent either from the quality of its adherents or the stubbornness of the facts it seeks to transform, to be worth sympathetic analysis, will do well to remember that in the early history of Christianity, the futility of its proponents and the folly of its doctrines probably seemed as obvious to the supporters of the Roman system.

It is, of course, a dangerous doctrine. Its application involves tremendous risks, even on the showing of communists themselves. If we assume the possibility of its success, the cost of establishing it would be enormously high; while an attempt that ended in failure might easily, by the scale of conflict it would arouse, come near to the destruction of civilised life. Neither prospect, it should be said at once, is any guarantee that the effort will not be made to give it application. As few doctrines in the world to-day, it commands a devoted service of which no man is entitled to underestimate the significance. Its adherents are not turned from their purpose either by imprisonment or death. In Germany and in Bulgaria, in Hungary and in the Far East, there is no danger they have not been willing to face in the desire to communicate their faith to others. They have the passionate zeal of the Jesuit missionary who sets out to conquer a new world for his creed.

The communist, moreover, is playing with combustible material. Even those who reject his principles must admit the large degree of truth in the indictment that he brings against the present social order. Neither our methods of production, nor our principles of distribution are capable of explanation in terms of social justice. The glaring inequalities that surround us on every side are hardly capable of overstatement. The liberation of the human spirit has not nearly kept pace with the conquest of nature by scientific discovery. The gain of living is denied to the majority of those who toil. And the more widely the realisation of these disparities is spread, the more intensely do men feel that they are intolerable. That is the more natural in the disillusion that follows upon a great war. Men feel that if they are to risk their lives for the State, its benefits should be proportionate to the danger.

It is in that mood of doubt that the masses meet the idealism of the communist faith. They hear an indictment of the conditions under which they live, which largely corresponds to their own experience. They are warned that they cannot trust to their rulers for the changes which will meet their needs. They are promised, in return for their energetic solidarity, an equal share in the gain of living as well as in its toil, a world in which there is principle instead of chaos, justice instead of privilege. To men whose environment is poisoned by insecurity, and for whom, in general, there is little hope of future benefit, the only wonder is that the promise has not proved more seductive.

Certainly, to counter its seduction means the alteration of the present social order by concessions larger in scope and profundity than any ruling class has so far been willing to make by voluntary act. It means allowing the democracy to have its way in every department of communal life, an acceptance, wholeheartedly, of Matthew Arnold's prescription, to "choose equality and flee greed." Yet it can hardly be denied that there are, in every community, groups of powerful men who make it a matter of principle to deny the validity of all concession. They display an ignorant hostility to change every whit as dangerous and provocative as the challenge they confront. They are as satisfied with the world about them, and as unconscious of its inadequacies, as the Duke of Wellington in 1832. They equate doubts of the world as it is with something like original sin; and they treat them with the same self-righteous cruelty as religions have in the past treated dissent from their announced principles. They feel, like General Cavaignac, that a social order which allows its principles to be examined, and, still more, rejected, is already lost. Their blindness drives the timid to despair and the bold to desperation. They are as unprepared for the politics of rational compromise as the most extreme of their opponents; and, by their obstinacy, they produce the very situation they desire to prevent. They do not see either the inevitability of large change, or the fact that it is desirable, and possible, to concert those changes in terms of the plain wants and needs of men. They talk of the rights of property as though these were some dread Absolute, instead of principles as shifting and inconstant as anything in the historic record. They arrogate to themselves liberty to deny while they refuse to their opponents liberty to affirm.

Yet the demands they confront do not

decrease in volume; and every arrest of their satisfaction is a victory for the forces of disruption. The only way to defeat these is to prove to their audience that you can the better respond to its wants and propose to do so. For we cannot postulate the basic identity of human nature and continue to refuse an adequate response to similar need. We can do it the less as men at once grow conscious of their powers and aware of the irrational differences in response to need.

It is thought by some that the dubious results of the Russian experiment, the cost, further, of what success it has won, will ultimately persuade men of the errors of communism. That, it may be suggested, is a mistaken calculation so long as there exist large classes of men and women who are conscious of inadequate and frustrated lives. The French Revolution lit flames in the hearts of mankind which, because it responded to something fundamental in human nature, neither its errors nor its crimes could quench. What the working-classes of the world see in Russia is less what its revolution denies than what it affirms. They see a State which, with all its faults and weaknesses, seems to them to lie at the service of men like themselves. They recognise in the demands it makes, and the principles to which it gives allegiance, their own demands and principles. We may admit that they are uncertain whether its gains outweigh the price paid for them; we may, also, agree that they resent the efforts of its leaders to force them to imitate the Russian example. But the indignation they display when (as in 1920) the security of Russia is challenged is evidence that, in an ultimate sense, the idea of the Russian Revolution stands for something of permanent value to them. The business man sees the inefficiency of Russian production; the worker sees the exaltation of the common man. The supporters of the old order warn the workers of the low level of wages, the discomfort of bad housing, the absence of political and intellectual freedom. To the workers, however, the things of import are the facts that all must toil, that communal experiment is in the interest of the masses, that no one is preferred save in terms of principle; and they have an uneasy suspicion that this atmosphere may largely compensate for the merits of the older way of life, so far as they share in them. The world, in fact, has to find response to the promise of communism in alternative forms; or it will discover that neither the crimes nor the follies of the Russian experiment will lessen its power to compel kindred action.

In a general sense, doubtless, the error of communism lies in its refusal to face the fact that this is a complex world. Its panacea is unreal simply because the world is too intricate for panaceas to have universal significance.

Any solution that is offered to our problems is bound, at its best and highest, to be but partial and imperfect; no single method of social arrangement will meet the diverse needs we encounter. That means, of course, that we need not, as communism offers us, the formulæ of conflict, but the formulæ of co-operation. The sceptical observer is unconvinced that any system has the future finally on its side; that it is entitled, from its certainties, to sacrifice all that has been acquired so painfully in the heritage of toleration and freedom, to the chance that its victory may one day compensate for a renunciation that, on its own admission, is bound to be grim and long. He has the more right to his scepticism both from the dissatisfaction with the economic dogmas of Marxism and from the knowledge of the cost which attends its application. He may admit the possibility that, in the end, the communist may prove right, even while he retains his doubt whether success implies the realisation of the ends he postulates. He may suspect whether any régime that is built on hate and fear and violence can give birth to an order rooted in fraternity. For these create an environment of which the children are, equally, hate and fear and violence. The spirit of man ever takes its revenge for degradation inflicted upon it even in the name of good.

But, whether we take the economic or the

political aspects of communism, it is far more important to grasp the truths it emphasises than to be merely denunciatory of the methods by which it seeks its ends. It was no answer to Luther to excommunicate him; the ignorant rhetoric of Burke hindered Europe rather than helped it in the understanding of 1789; and those who have sought the destruction of the new Russia have only added to, and not subtracted from, the problems of our generation. That a wide distribution of political power is worthless unless there is a similar distribution of economic power; that there can be no effective moral unity in a State divided, in Disraeli's phrase, into the two nations of rich and poor; that the absence of such unity means a violent attempt to destroy, and a violent attempt to preserve, any social order so distinguished; that men think differently who live differently and, so thinking, lose their sense of kinship through the frustration of impulse; these are the obvious commonplaces of history. Nor is it possible to deny that, with the general tendency of governments to degenerate the lesson of experience is the continuous need to preserve by associating the widest interests with the benefits conferred by social systems. But that means a thoroughgoing reform in the direction of widening the basis of effective consent. Effective consent, in its turn, means the revision of the rights of property towards an equality greater than we have so far known; for in no other fashion can we obtain that equalisation of privilege which has become the purpose of the modern State.[1]

This is, clearly enough, to argue that it is possible and desirable to attain the ultimate aims of communism by alternative paths. And this, in a broad way, will be accepted by all who remain dissatisfied both with the achievement of capitalism and the motives upon which it rests. The compelling strength of communism is that it has a faith as vigorous, as fanatic, and compelling as any in the history of religions. It offers dogmas to those whom scepticism troubles; it brings to its believers the certitude which all great religions have conferred; above all, perhaps, it implants in its adherents the belief in their ultimate redemption. If it is said that, like other religions, it destroys and persecutes, it can make the answer—which mankind has always found a convincing answer—that it destroys and persecutes in the name of truth. It is fatal to underestimate the strength of this temper. It is the thing that moved the early Christians, the Puritans of the seventeenth century, the legions of Mahomet, to victory, against obstacles which must have seemed insuperable to their contemporaries. To those who do not accept it, it may seem a

[1] Cf. my *Grammar of Politics*, Chaps. VI and VII, for an amplification of this view.

joyless creed which takes from life its colour, and a relentless creed which takes from the hearts of men the sovereign virtues of charity and justice. But to such an attitude there are at least two answers. The Puritan creed did not seem joyless to those who embraced it; on the contrary, there was for its devotees a splendour in its stern renunciation more emotionally complete than any other experience it was possible to know; and when the mind, secondly, becomes possessed of a truth it believes to be exclusive, it no longer admits that charity and justice are sovereign virtues.

"Its emotional and ethical essence," writes Mr. Keynes of communism, "centres about the individual's and the community's attitude to money . . . it tries to construct a framework of society in which pecuniary motives as influencing action shall have a changed relative importance, in which social approbations shall be differently distributed, and where behaviour which previously was normal and respectable, ceases to be either the one or the other." This is a transvaluation of values in the degree that is the essence of religious faith. And it is worth while observing that, with all its difficulties, it has an enormous psychological appeal. The idealism of youth responds to it. It is of that inner citadel of conviction which moves the artist, the poet, the scientist, the philosopher, to their achievement. It is the mark which distinguishes those historic gestures which, as in St. Francis or Savonarola, or George Fox, have given great leaders the power to command the loyalties of men. Even its partial success would make an epoch in the history of the world, and, even if it prove Utopian, it is clearly an ideal both high enough and intense enough to win from those who accept it the ultimate service of heart and mind.

One cannot help insisting upon this aspect of communism because its implications are what primarily strikes the detached observer who comes into contact with it. Its power to communicate the will to serve, its sense of exhilaration through contact with high purpose, its ability to make all alien from itself seem mean and unimportant, these, certainly, are beyond discussion. It gives something of the mental and moral excitement that is felt by the reader of the poetry inspired by the French Revolution, the unconquerable hope, the heedless and instinctive generosity, which makes great ends seem worth working for because they are attainable by ourselves. Most Europeans had something of that sense when the news came of the first Russian Revolution in March of 1917; it brought to them a new elasticity of mind which made the effort of victory seem emotionally easier. Most Englishmen had it again in the days after the Armistice of 1918 when it seemed possible to transfer the comradeship of co-operation in war to the days of peace.

The question that this raises for ourselves is whether capitalism is likely to inspire in the hearts of even those who live by its results emotions of similar intensity. We live in a civilisation which avowedly separates its economic practice from its religious and moral faith. That means that its economic practice must, as Mr. Keynes has pointed out, be enormously successful if it is to survive. It must be able to leave men so circumstanced that there is room in the lives of the rank and file as well as of leaders to be ends for themselves as well as means through which others move to their appointed purpose. In no other fashion can the capitalistic system win the loyalty of the mass. It is no longer either optimistic or self-confident as it was in the days of Nassau Senior and McCulloch. It acts, in almost every sphere, as a body of ideas and practices that is permanently on the defensive. It is significant, for instance, that whereas a hundred years ago it did not have to square its accounts with the Churches, because these were prostrate before its achievement, to-day the Churches increasingly insist that the economic system must be judged in terms of their religious message. It is significant because the ultimate dogma of the Churches is the conviction of the basic equality of men. And for those increasing numbers to whom official religions of all kinds make little or no moral appeal, capitalism, certainly, has nothing of spiritual significance to offer. The Puritan could be hard and grim in riches or poverty because his real life was not of this world. But those who lack the conviction such confidence brings will not be content with an economic system which limits to so few the possibility of an inner harmony. That is why, it may be urged, there are so many Russians who regard the economic failures of the Revolution as insignificant alongside the spiritual liberation it has brought them. And it is not improbable that others, weary of material failure and spiritual inertia, may be persuaded, with all its dangers, to think likewise.

Therein, certainly, is the lesson that the communist theory enforces; and we have either to learn that lesson in other ways or to admit the prospect that no means of avoiding its consequences are at our disposal. Communism has made its way by its idealism and not its realism, by its spiritual promise, not its materialistic prospect. It is a creed in which there is intellectual error, moral blindness, social perversity. Religions make their way despite these things. Mankind in history has been amazingly responsive to any creed which builds its temple upon spiritual heights. The answer to the new faith is not the persecution of those who worship in its sanctuary, but the proof that those who do not share its convictions can scan an horizon not less splendid in the prospect it envisions nor less compelling in the allegiance it invokes.

BIBLIOGRAPHY

1. On communism in antiquity the best work is Pohlman, *Geschicte des antiken communismus* ; on the communism of the Middle Ages Fr. Bede Jarrett's *Medieval Socialism* and his *Social Theories of the Middle Ages* are both excellent; on Sir Thomas More, see his *Utopia* (ed. Lupton) and the studies of this by Kautsky and Oncken; on Winstanley the best book is by L. H. Berens, *The Digger Movement.* On French socialism in the eighteenth century Lichtenberger, *Le Socialisme Français au xviiime Siècle* is admirable; on the nineteenth century up to the emergence of Marx the best work is G. Isambert, *Les Idées Socialistes au* 1848. On early English socialism the *History* by M. Beer is of high value.

2. There is as yet no collected edition of Marx's writings; though one is to be published by the Marx-Lenin Institute. The following, in chronological order, is a list of his principal works: *The Holy Family* (1845), (with Engels); the *Misery of Philosophy* (1847); *The Communist Manifesto* (1848), (with Engels); *The Eighteenth Brumaire* (1850); *Palmerston, what has he done ?* (1855); *Critique of Political Economy* (1859); *Herr Vogt* (1860); *Capital,* Vol I. (1867) (the sole volume published in his lifetime; Vols. II. and III. were edited after his death by Engels); *Letters on the Gotha Program* (1875); *The Civil War in France* (1891); *Class Struggles in France,* 1848–50 (1895); *Revolution and Counter-Revolution* (1896); *The Eastern Question* (1897); *Wages, Labour and Capital* (1908); *Value, Price and Profit* (1908). Material of great value will be found in two German collections: (1) *Aus dem literarischen Nachlass von K. Marx und Fr. Engels,* 1841–50, ed. Mehring, 2 vols.; (2) *Der Briefwechsel zwischen Engels und Marx,* ed. Bebel and Bernstein, 4 vols. The standard life of Marx is by F. Mehring; in English, the best biography is that of M. Beer.

3. N. Lenin :

**The State and Revolution.*
**The Proletarian Revolution.*
**The Infantile Malady of Communism.*
**Imperialism, The Last Phase of Capitalism.*
**Will the Bolsheviks maintain Power ?*
**The Soviets at Work.*
**On the Road to Insurrection.*
What, then, shall we do ?
The Bolsheviks and the Peasants.
The Soviets and Women.

L. Trotsky :

**Terrorism and Communism.*
**The Defence of Terrorism.*
*1905.
**The Lessons of October* 1917.
The Paris Commune and Soviet Russia.
The Crisis in French Communism.
**Where is Britain going ?*

G. Zinoviev :

The Tactics of the United Front.
The History of the Russian Communist Party.
The Communist Party at Work.
International Perspectives and the Bolshevisation of Parties.
The Essential Traits of the Present Period.
N. Lenin.

Stalin :

Questions and Answers.
Leninism in Theory and Practice.

N. Bukharin :

**A B C of Communism.*

E. Varga :

The Dictatorship of the Proletariat.

[Reports of Congresses of the Third International, especially the reports and programmes of the Fifth World Congress, and its monthly organ (published in English as *The Communist International*), are of great value. Here will be found its statutes and theses as they vary with the changing world situation. Extracts from some of them are published in English by the Communist Party of Great Britain.]

Of the books by Russian Communists listed above, those marked with an asterisk have been translated into English.

4. A. Rothstein (ed.): *The Soviet Constitution.*

R. W. Postgate: *The Workers' International* (the best existing account).

Various: *The Second and Third Internationals and the Vienna Union.*

Ernest Drahn: *Lenin* (the best bibliography; in German).

W. Paul: *Communism and Society.*

W. Paul: *The State.*

Bertrand Russell: *The Theory and Practice of Bolshevism.*

H. N. Brailsford: *The Soviet Workers' Republic.*

The first part of Mr. H. G. Wells' *World of William Clissold* contains a characteristically brilliant, if sometimes perverse, picture of Marxian Socialism.

The above are, it should be insisted, only a handful of the more representative discussions; but they will at least serve to introduce the reader to the problem.

H. J. L.

INDEX

Printed in Great Britain by Butler & Tanner Ltd., Frome and London

HISTORY—(*continued*)

The Papacy and Modern Times	Rev. Dr. W. Barry
History of our Time, 1885–1913	G. P. Gooch, M.A.
The Civilisation of China	Prof. H. A. Giles, LL.D.
Dawn of History	Prof. J. L. Myres
The History of England: A Study in Political Evolution	Prof. A. F. Pollard
Canada	A. G. Bradley
Peoples and Problems of India	Sir T. W. Holderness
Rome	W. Warde Fowler, M.A.
The American Civil War (Maps)	Prof. F. L. Paxson
Warfare in England (Maps)	Hilaire Belloc, M.A.
Master Mariners	J. R. Spears
Napoleon (Maps)	Rt. Hon. H. A. L. Fisher, M.P., LL.D.
The Navy and Sea Power	David Hannay
Germany of To-day	Charles Tower
Pre-Historic Britain	Dr. Robert Munro
The Ancient East	D. G. Hogarth, F.B.A.
Wars between England and America	Prof. T. C. Smith
History of Scotland	Prof. R. S. Rait
Belgium (Maps)	R. C. K. Ensor
Poland (Maps)	Prof. W. Alison Phillips
Serbia	L. F. Waring, B.A.
Our Forerunners	M. C. Burkitt, M.A., F.S.A.
Wales	W. Watkin Davies, F.R.Hist.S.
Egypt (Illustrated)	Sir E. A. Wallis Budge, M.A.
The Byzantine Empire	Norman H. Baynes
England under the Tudors and Stuarts	Keith Feiling, M.A.
History of England, 1688–1815	E. M. Wrong, M.A.
The Civilisation of Japan	J. Ingram Bryan, M.A., M.Litt.

LITERATURE

2. Shakespeare	John Masefield
5. The Civilisation of China	Prof. H. A. Giles, LL.D.
7. English Literature: Modern	George Mair, M.A.
5. Landmarks in French Literature	Lytton Strachey
3. English Literature: Mediæval	Prof. W. P. Ker
5. The English Language	L. Pearsall Smith
2. Great Writers of America	Profs. W. P. Trent and J. Erskine
4. Dr. Johnson and his Circle	John Bailey, M.A.
5. The Literature of Germany	Prof. J. G. Robertson, M.A.
0. The Victorian Age in Literature	G. K. Chesterton
3. The Writing of English	Prof. W. T. Brewster
6. Euripides and his Age	Gilbert Murray, LL.D.
7. Shelley, Godwin and their Circle	H. N. Brailsford, M.A.
7. Chaucer and his Times	Grace Hadow
9. William Morris	A. Clutton Brock
5. Elizabethan Literature	J. M. Robertson, M.P.

LITERATURE—(*continued*)

POLITICAL & SOCIAL SCIENCE

RELIGION & PHILOSOPHY

SCIENCE

SCIENCE—(*continued*)